RENOVATION
BOOTCAMP:™
KITCHEN

DESIGN AND REMODEL YOUR KITCHEN...
WITHOUT LOSING YOUR WALLET, YOUR MIND OR YOUR SPOUSE.

Robin Siegerman
Foreword by Steve Thomas
Cartoons by Andy Donato

Yorkshire Publishing Company

Renovation Boot Camp™: Kitchen
Design and Remodel Your Kitchen... Without Losing Your Wallet,
Your Mind or Your Spouse
April Edit 2011

ISBN: 978-0-88144-502-2
Copyright © 2011 by Robin Siegerman

Published by
Yorkshire Publishing
9731 East 54th Street
Tulsa, OK 74146
www.yorkshirepublishing.com

WHAT THEY'VE SAID ABOUT:

Renovation Bootcamp™: Kitchen:

"Step away from that tape measure, put down the hammer, and don't dial that designer until you've read Renovation Bootcamp from cover to cover! This book demystifies and deescalates everything that is fraught and frightening about kitchen renos. It's like having a first class designer at your beck and call, what a bargain!"

– Teresa Toten, Award-Winning Author

teresatoten.com

"Don't even think about remodelling your kitchen before you read this book! Robin Siegerman has written a user-friendly, upbeat, fun to read book with loads of great photos and amusing anecdotes, checklists, and questionnaires. Get all the answers before you're up to your neck in drywall dust! I wish I had read Renovation Bootcamp before I renovated my last kitchen, but you can bet I'll keep it handy for my NEXT remodel!"

– Peggy McColl, New York Times Best-Selling Author

"When I remodel my kitchen, Robin Siegerman's Renovation Bootcamp: Kitchen will be my guide. Her book is gutsy, practical, and nicely written. She steers her reader through the sometimes messy nightmare that is renovation. Her sage advice has even saved a marriage or two."

– Maggie Siggins, author and filmmaker

"Robin Siegerman takes the profession of interior design seriously and shares that passion with eager readers. While her boot camp won't get you in better physical condition, it will prepare you for the rigors of renovating. It's a luxury to hire a professional designer; if that's not an option you'll be happy to have Robin's book on your team."

– Kimberley Seldon, Interior Designer, author, journalist,
keynote speaker, and broadcast personality

"As producer of HGTV's hit show Real Reno's, I have had the pleasure of having Robin Siegerman on our show many times as both designer and homeowner. Her wonderful sense of design, humour, and ability to connect to her clients and our viewers has made her an excellent addition to the show. She's a refreshing straight-shooter....no design diva here. While renovations that go wrong make for great television, a reno does not have to be a disaster, but only if homeowners know what to expect. A guide by a pro like Robin would be invaluable. She knows all the pitfalls and how to avoid them. This guide could save you money, aggravation, and maybe your relationship."
– Linda McEwan, Smashing Pictures

"Robin's advice is as useful as her designs are beautiful. Practical, personable, and often very funny, she never fails to both entertain and inform. I wish her book had been around when I was renovating."
– Leslee Mason, Editor, Canadian Kitchen and Bath

Robin's columns, articles, and radio interviews:

"[It's] no surprise that you've developed the following of readers that you have. There's something about having the ability (and the guts) to tell it like it is. I really enjoy the read."
– Adam Freill, Editor, Mechanical Business

"I wanted to let you know how much I enjoy your articles. It is comforting to know that I am not alone in my experiences and it is great to hear it from another designer who likes to tell it like it is. Please keep it up."
– Lisa Geisler, Designer/Proprietor, Creative Interiors, Powassan, ON

"Just read the Spring issue of C K&B. Great article you wrote. I have been frustrated by just this topic for many years. About time someone came out and said so."
– Frank Siekmann, President, Merit Kitchens, Surrey, BC

"Thanks for joining me on the radio. The interview was informative and interesting. My listeners got a lot of practical tips from you, and now know the differences between interior designers, architects, and decorators. Keep up the good work!"
– Shep Cohen, WDVRFM Radio, Newark, N.J.

"You and I see things so similarly... When one designer tells you something that's great, but when two designers say exactly the same thing independently of one another, you can take that to the bank. I can't believe how fast a one hour interview flew by! I enjoyed talking to you, thank you!"
   – Natalie Weinstein, Interior Designer and Host, WALK 97.5 Radio, Long Island, NY

"As a manufacturer it was a treat to read your article and your bold opinion on the sometimes overlooked blended design and sales expertise of those in the kitchen industry. Robin, thank you for writing this article, it was a good read and please keep this type of insight flowing."
   – Bob Wiens, V.P. Sales & Marketing Elmwood Kitchens, St. Catharines, ON

Robin's Design Work

"I can't count the number of people who've said to us, "this is one of the nicest kitchens I've ever been in." We had business-related guests join us for a casual dinner over the holidays. I offered to serve coffee and dessert in our drawing room and they said they wanted to "stay put" in the kitchen as they liked it so much. Robin knows her stuff. She's great to work with. She's worth every penny."
   – Deborah Thompson, Toronto, ON

"Robin took our ideas for our new kitchen and guided us through the design process with her friendly and confident manner. She has an aesthetic that seems to be able to adjust to client taste.... Robin was generous with her considerable knowledge, and with her time and talents.... Her attention to detail, combined with her design skills and aesthetic helped us achieve an excellent result – we don't just enjoy cooking in our new kitchen, we enjoy and are proud to entertain friends and family there."
   – Carla Rinaldo and Virginia Walley, Peterborough, ON

"I can't say enough about how pleased we are with our new kitchen. The design that you prepared and executed accomplished our two key goals for the room – providing us with a highly functional kitchen for use by the family while concurrently respecting the strong historic character of the overall home. There is nothing that we have found about the room that we would change."
   – Roger Dent and Susan Lambie, Toronto, ON

TABLE OF CONTENTS

FOREWORD

I met Robin about 15 years ago on a ski slope. She was brash and opinionated then and the intervening decade and a half has not changed her much. You might think this is a negative when it comes to kitchen design, but it's not!

Let me explain.

The kitchen is the most highly designed, heavily engineered, and intensely built room of the house. Square foot for square foot it is the most expensive, the most difficult to design and the hardest to change once it is built. Aside from our sleeping hours in the bedroom, it is where we spend the most time with our friends and family. In all respects, the kitchen remains the heart of the house – how many times have you tried to shoo your 10 or 12 dinner guests out of the kitchen and back into the dining room? Every piece of "furniture" in the kitchen, cabinets, plumbing fixtures, and appliances, require careful consideration, cost a lot of money, and once screwed to the walls, they can't be moved! In other words, you have only one chance to get it right, which is in the design phase.

The kitchen is first and foremost a workshop, so it has to be practical, sturdy, well-lit, easy to keep clean, and as functional for making an omelet for one as it is to prepare a holiday feast for 20. And, given that we do everything in our kitchens, from sipping our morning coffee while answering our e-mail, to making kids' lunches, supervising homework, and entertaining our friends, it has to be a supple, versatile, beautiful space. No other room in the house has such a demanding set of design standards. Get it right and you'll enjoy your kitchen every day for the next 20 years. Get it wrong and you'll be kicking yourself for the next 20 years!

Robin designed a kitchen for my wife and I a number of years ago when we were about to re-renovate our 10-year-old kitchen in our historic home in the Boston area. For a variety of reasons, we never got up the courage to do the renovation, and from then until we recently sold the house, we regretted it. The number of choices in kitchen materials has exploded in recent years, from lighting fixtures, to appliances, flooring surfaces, countertops, plumbing fixtures, and heating and cooling options. To choose from among them in a way that reflects your style, budget, and the primary purpose of your kitchen takes a guide with a confident sense of direction.

Robin is a kitchen designer, yes, but she's primarily a guide, leading you through the wilderness of expensive and confusing kitchen design choices with a strong opinion of her own, a great knowledge of the field, and yes, a sense of humor! This book will help you design the kitchen you really want on a budget you can afford and keep your marriage intact while doing so!

I look forward to my next kitchen renovation. We'll have Robin design it, and this time, I'll actually build it!

Steve Thomas
Former Host of *This Old House*, on PBS
Former Producer & Host Renovation Nation on Discovery's Planet Green

INTRODUCTION

Renovating a kitchen is an emotional business. It is arguably the most important room in the house. A kitchen is to a home what air traffic control is to an airport; what mission control is to NASA; what the hub is to a transportation line; what the heart is to the body. A deeply personal space, it can be the scene of domestic intimacy, creativity, harmony, and even drama and discord within the family. Most families make their most important decisions sitting around the kitchen table. Therefore, it's essential that homeowners contemplating a kitchen renovation are prepared with an unvarnished account of what to expect. Foresight will save time, money, and sanity.

If you've ever contemplated a kitchen renovation but gotten stalled when confronted with the hundreds of choices and decisions, this book is for you. If you've ever agonized over who is best equipped to create your kitchen design, an architect, an interior designer, or a kitchen professional, this book will give you the answers. If you are overwhelmed by the sheer number of cabinet styles, materials, finishes, flooring, countertops, tiles, appliances, colors, and lighting choices, this book will help demystify the selection process. You can finally tune out the gobbledygook of conflicting opinions of friends, family, well-meaning neighbors, and other self-appointed "experts" who may or may not have ever even done a renovation.

Over the past 19 years in my work as a Registered Interior Designer and award-winning Certified Kitchen Designer, I've noticed consumers have become increasingly aware of the myriad of style and product choices available: traditional, contemporary, transitional style; painted, stained, lacquered, or laminate cabinets; marble, granite, quartz, solid surface, and laminate countertops; and dozens of other types of equipment, fixtures, materials, and finishes that contribute to a completed kitchen.

Unfortunately, while clients often come to my office clutching a file, bag, or box of magazine clippings vividly illustrating their aesthetic preferences, they are mired in utter confusion and discord about the process of renovating a kitchen. Often, one spouse is convinced that they need to do "A," the other spouse is equally convinced that "B" is the correct course, and I end up being part marriage counsellor as well as designer and renovation coordinator.

In my experience, articles and books on kitchen renovation underestimate the costs, detailed design and planning required, the time it will take, and downplay the challenges likely to arise along the way.

Renovation is not an exact science. Unforeseen and unavoidable delays add extra costs. When you know the potential worst case scenario upfront, you will be psychologically prepared if the worst actually does happen. If things go better than that, everyone will be happy, including all the tradespeople working on your project. No one wants their clients to be unhappy. Sometimes a contractor, designer, or kitchen cabinet sales person is so anxious to make you happy, they will underestimate costs or the time required to complete a job—setting up a scenario where the customer's inflated expectations are destined to end in disappointment and frustration, ultimately reflecting poorly on an entire industry. My role, for better or worse, is to tell you the truth, the whole truth, and yadda, yadda, yadda, so you won't be blind-sided by the inevitable challenges you'll face.

My clients typically spend $100,000 or more to renovate their kitchen. They know a beautifully designed kitchen with high-quality materials and finishes will add value to their home, and most importantly, improve their family's quality of life. (If you renovate properly and sell within a certain period of time, you can recoup 85%-100% of your investment. I will come back to what "properly" actually means later on in the book.) But my clients also have high expectations, and why not? For that kind of money, you should be able to expect a perfect renovation with no problems, right? WRONG!

Whether you're spending $10,000 on a minor kitchen facelift or $200,000 or more on a complete overhaul, the potential pitfalls are the same: the most probable of which is human frailty. Even the most celebrated designers, the most expensive cabinet manufacturers, and the most experienced contractors occasionally make mistakes. Sometimes, one mistake or one missed deadline can set off a chain reaction that causes weeks of delay and hours of time to coordinate a solution to get the project back on track. If the project was poorly planned, missing essential details before it starts, often the quagmire of problems that result will multiply exponentially and end up costing you extra money, time, and great aggravation.

This book will explain each major step in the process and how to plan your remodel, right down to all the minor components, to help you forestall the challenges and frustrations that may come up. Armed with the information in this book, you will be able to spot problems early enough to correct them, before there's too much delay, saving you time, money, your sanity, and possibly your marriage. The only thing I can't promise you is a perfect renovation and a perfect marriage. I'm good, but magic isn't part of the act!

TALES FROM THE TRENCHES

Some people think I'm seriously deranged when I mention a figure of $100,000 to remodel a kitchen as I did earlier. I can understand how you'd think that. But consider your last car purchase. If you bought a luxury car like a Lexus with all the bells and whistles, you might expect to spend approximately $70,000 plus freight and taxes. If you are a luxury car customer, you will probably keep your car four years. Which is a better deal? The $100,000 kitchen you will keep for 20 years or the $70,000 car you'll keep for four? Even if you are not a luxury car or kitchen customer, the same equation applies. When you start considering the price of a new kitchen including new appliances, flooring, cabinets, countertops and lighting, and the fact that your family and friends will gather there for many more years than you expect to keep your car even if you do drive it into the ground, think of my car analogy and the price will be easier to understand.

RULES OF ENGAGEMENT

Here's an overview of the cardinal rules to follow for a successful renovation.
I will explain each in detail later:

1 Don't play the "guess my budget" game.

Be fair to your designer/contractor/cabinet supplier. Know what you can afford to spend and how you will finance the project before you start to plan a design. First and foremost, a designer needs to know your budget. Designing without a budget is like believing you really can get to Kansas by clicking your heels. Dumb, right? But you'd be surprised how many people hope and fantasize that a designer can magically design a kitchen that looks like a feature in Architectural Digest for less than the cost of a used station wagon. They seem to think that as long as they pretend it's possible, perhaps it can be so.

2 You get what you pay for.

If the price is too good to be true, be suspicious.

3 Design your kitchen to your taste.

Honestly, if I had a hundred dollars for every client who told me they wanted a kitchen that would never go out of style and that would appeal to every potential buyer for resale I'd be on a tropical island right now sipping a mai-tai. Unless you plan to sell your home in the next 18 months to three years, or you know in your heart you may be forced to sell and a renovation is strictly to help the sale, just go ahead and have it designed to your taste. No matter which style you choose, it won't appeal to everyone, but someone will love it. If you expect your remodel to pay off when you resell in ten years, forget it. After a decade of day-to-day use, the place will look dated and tired. A good designer will translate your personality and preferences into a three-dimensional, real-life kitchen you love.

4 Don't leave town!

During most renovations, at least one or two things will crop up that need your input and approval. To go away with the kids for a summer escape and expect to return home to an on time, under budget, sparkling new kitchen, is foolhardy. If you leave someone else in charge, you may return to find modifications and extra costs you didn't expect. Don't blame the contractor. You weren't there.

5 Keep your sense of humor & a balanced perspective.

When you've ordered yet another take out meal, and guys in boots tromp through your house eight hours a day, it's hard to be patient. When challenges arise, and the remedy appears delayed unnecessarily, please realize you will never have the whole picture. You can't know the entire chain of events required to resolve a problem. Sometimes what seems like a straightforward remedy can entail several phone calls, order processing, manufacturing queues, and shipping logistics, all of which consume time and challenge your patience. But if you are able to keep your sense of humor and a balanced perspective, you will enjoy the end result so much more when it's done.

6 Threats don't work.

Okay, well that's not entirely true, but when your last nerve is fried and you can't remember what life was like without drywall dust, and things just don't seem to be moving along as fast as you think they should, threatening to withhold or dock payment won't do much more than make your contractor mutter something rude and take an extra long lunch. Earlier in my career, I got triggered and was about to blast off on some poor soul and really let him have it, and a very wise country lawyer told me, "Yep, well, you could do that...but I've always found you can attract a lot more bees with honey than with vinegar."
Very smart guy.

Now, keeping these rules in mind let the remodeling begin!

Before and After

Removing a structural wall to improve flow and function may require support posts. Whenever possible, try to incorporate them into the design. Be sure to get the required structural drawings and permits first

Planning is Key

Is it a Facelift or Reconstructive Surgery?

part one

PLANNING IS KEY

Do You Need a Facelift or Reconstructive Surgery?

Food for thought:

Some contractors really ARE a little sketchy. An electrician I once worked with was suspected of wiretapping.

Do you have to blow out the kitchen and relocate it to another part of the house to create enough working space, an eating area, and get a second oven, or is the reality that you only can afford a new coat of paint, a new faucet, and an updated light fixture?

Before you get excited and start spending your weekends shopping for cabinets and countertops for your kitchen renovation, take some time to make some key decisions that will save hours of your precious time, minimize your aggravation, and limit your disappointment.

This kitchen modification could be considered a face-lift rather than a full scale remodel since no new cabinets were added and the location of the plumbing didn't change.

What was removed: The counter top, peninsula cabinets, floor, backsplash tiles, appliances, sink & faucet.

What was done: Existing cabinets left over were painted and had a crown moulding added, new floor, backsplash tile, laminate counter, sink, faucet, stainless steel appliances, and a store-bought stainless steel island piece with stools. This kind of facelift is worth doing if you want to do a major renovation, but need to wait for several years before you do it. It will make the kitchen a happier place in the meantime.

Take an objective view of your home and ask yourself:

- Do you expect to sell this house in the next three to five years? Or is this your "forever" home?
- Do the property values in your neighborhood tend to trend upward, even in the last five years?
- Is there typically a lot of remodelling or knock-down and re-construction going on in your area?
- Is your house on a decent piece of property, in a good location in your town, suburb, or city?
- Do you like the neighborhood and the amenities nearby?
- Would a major renovation of your kitchen make you feel better about your house and make daily meal preparation more enjoyable or at least less stressful?
- Are you securely employed, and do you have good credit and a means to obtain financing that won't cause you undue hardship?

TALES FROM THE TRENCHES

Before we moved to a new home in a different part of town, I really had no idea what we were giving up. In our new home, I was looking forward to living closer to downtown, my son's school and my ailing father. I was shocked to learn not every neighborhood is as nice a community as the one we left. On our old block, neighbors organized a street sale every summer which ended with a big barbeque in someone's backyard; we got together each year for a Christmas cocktail party. One of my neighbors even threw a baby shower for me. We've lived in our new neighborhood for 11 years. Here, there is very little interaction between homeowners; no animosity, mostly just indifference, and the impact on our quality of life is palpable. If you're thinking about moving rather than going through the hassle and expense of a renovation, I would strongly urge you to weigh the pros and cons of each. Chances are, even if you move, you will have to spend money fixing up the new house, and you may leave behind some wonderful neighborhood qualities that you didn't even realize you had 'til they're gone.

If you answered yes to three or more of the above questions, you are a candidate for a full remodel. A renovation can provide you with a kitchen that is a joy to work in and is a place you'll want to open to friends and extended family. When I renovated several years ago, the kitchen was just one piece of a whole home remodeling project. But we enjoy the new kitchen so much; some of the other rooms are used way less than before. In the morning, we go from the bedroom to the kitchen and out the door to work, and we come home into the kitchen and stay there until it's almost time to go to bed again! My clients repeatedly report a similar experience.

If you're happy in your neighborhood, you get along well with your neighbors, you love the schools, shops, and restaurants nearby, it's well worth renovating your house and staying in it over a longer period. The financial and emotional costs of relocating can be higher than you think, especially if you end up in a beautiful house in a less friendly neighborhood.

If, on the other hand, your answers to my earlier questions were an overwhelming "no," perhaps the following questions are more likely to elicit "yes" responses.
Are you unhappy with the neighborhood or location of your home?
Do you see this as a house that you are likely to sell in the next year or so?
Are the housing prices in your area typically stagnant, without much upward movement, even in good economic times?
If you invest in a new kitchen for your home, will adding the cost of a renovation mean your sale price would need to far exceed the value of comparable homes in the area?
Is your employment situation unpredictable, your credit shaky, or your financial situation less secure than you would like?
Are you less than thrilled with the schools or amenities in your neighborhood?

If you answered "yes" to three out of five of these, you may be better off to keep your kitchen upgrade investment to a minimum. If the room is dreary and depressing, you can make minor cosmetic changes, like the photo on page 1, that will help you feel better in the space until you move or are able to afford a more substantial renovation. Start with the walls and ceilings. It's amazing how much better you'll feel when you add a couple of coats of fresh paint. If the cabinets would benefit from painting, please do it properly. A poorly done paint job can be almost as ugly as dreary cabinets in their original finish. Take the doors off the cabinets, sand them down, and use a really good primer. To simplify clean up and minimize toxic fumes, you can use a water-based paint, but make sure it's a semi-gloss finish to resist fingerprints and provide easy clean up when smudges do appear.

W Studio

If long term plans include living in the home for ten years or more, it's worth the expense to do a full scale renovation with good quality materials.

HOW MUCH WILL IT COST?

Food for thought:

The four most expensive words in renovation are:

While. We're. At. It.

ven when you know your budget, many decisions need to be made before we can determine the actual price tag for the renovation.

Consider:

- How many cabinets will there be? What you have now is not necessarily the same number you will have in a new design.
- What is the overall cabinet height, door style, finish? Is it a stain, or paint with a glaze, or lacquer? If you're contemplating cabinetry from a big box store, you might be able to get a linear foot price on cabinets, countertop material, and installation before you begin. However, since they are not custom cabinets, you'll have limited choices of finish and sizes, and they are usually of a basic quality. That being said, they are a good solution if your budget is tight, and you're trying to stretch each dollar as far as you can.
- Will there be glass inserts in the doors and will the glass be clear, frosted, textured, seeded, stained, or antique?
- Which wood species do you plan to use?
- What type of internal accessories do you want, i.e. cutlery trays, knife blocks, roll out shelves, food processor lift, spice storage, towel bars, trash/recycling/compost containers?
- What style of crown moulding and light valance will you use? How many lengths?
- What finish will the toe kick (the panel underneath the base cabinets that meets the floor) be? And how many lengths will be required?
- What style cabinet pulls (knobs or handles) do you want? The labor costs to install them on the job site are different for each type.

- What material do you want for your countertops: granite, marble, quartz, laminate, solid surface?
- What's your preference for edge profile? Choices include square, waterfall, ogee, bullnose, and a bunch of others.
- What brand of appliances, which items and which colors will you choose? Typically stainless steel costs more than white and a cabinet-match panel is even more expensive and requires labor to install the panels.
- What brand and size of sink would you like?
- How about the finish and brand of faucet?
- Will you want a TV in the kitchen, and will it be wall-mounted, under-cabinet mounted, on a shelf, or in a cabinet?
- Will there be a built-in sound system and speakers?
- What kind of material do you envision on the backsplash (the wall area between the counter top and the underside of the wall cabinets)?
- If the backsplash will be tile, will it be ceramic, porcelain, stone, glass, wood, or laminate?
- What about flooring?
- What type of lighting? How many fixtures and what kind of bulbs will be needed?
- Will the new lighting require removing the whole ceiling to run new wiring?
- Will the walls be painted or will there be a wall covering like tile, paper, or vinyl?
- Are new windows or doors required?
- Are window coverings required, and if so, will they be blinds, shutters, fabric drapes, or shades? Will there be a valance?
- What kind of table and how many chairs will you need?

Do you now see why it's impossible to get an exact price for your kitchen before all these decisions are made? Your kitchen designer can advise you and help come up with the most appropriate answers, but many of these questions cannot be answered until after the design is done. To work within your budget, make a prioritized wish list of what you'd ideally like to have, then let your designer guide you as to what you can have and stay within your budget.

Armed with a budget you can afford, you can interview various design and remodeling professionals and ask them if they can work within your budget. Some people are embarrassed to talk about money, yet there is no shame in having a modest budget. If someone walked into my office and told me they had a total of $10,000 to spend, I would suggest they visit a big box store instead, since my particular company caters to the upper middle end of the market. When you establish the financial parameters up front and discuss your budget honestly and openly from the beginning, you'll save everyone a lot of time and frustration and get a kitchen you can comfortably afford.

When you conduct your interviews, find out if the interior designers and contractors you talk to actually have expertise in kitchen design. A CKD (Certified Kitchen Designer) has passed a national exam to test competency and knowledge of kitchen design principles, construction requirements, and safety issues. Ask them to provide a price range of what their average kitchen renovation costs, so you will know if their range falls within your budget. Similarly, if your budget exceeds $100,000, you'll want to ensure that the design and remodeling professionals you hire have the expertise to fulfill your wish list.

You may be thinking, "$100,000 to remodel a kitchen? What's that lady smoking?" Lest you believe that I must be ingesting some mind-altering substance to suggest a budget of $100,000, let me run through the costs of a typical, mid-sized kitchen renovation, item by item, so you can see where I got that number. The numbers will vary depending on the locality, currency values, the economic climate, and sometimes the season. A lot of pricing variations boil down to supply and demand. But you can also use this list to call vendors to get your own pricing, so you can come up with a ball-park budget.

The Nitty-Gritty of Cost

Regional differences will certainly affect the cost of materials, but location will mostly influence labor costs. Typically, rural tradespeople charge less than their urban counterparts and labor in the larger cities is priced higher than smaller ones. The best way to get a sense of costs in your area is to refer to real estate costs relative to other parts of the country.

I designed and renovated a simple kitchen without too many design or product frills for a four bedroom house located in a suburb. The kitchen was about 12' wide by 25' long and included an eating area for six people. None of the prices include installation, delivery, and tax, all of which vary widely from region to region.

A simple kitchen layout will vary in cost depending on the quality of materials and labor

After checking the order three times and verifying the written confirmation, manufacturing mistakes can still happen, causing unanticipated delays.

The plan below will serve as an example for pricing purposes to illustrate the items that need to be included to get an accurate project quote.

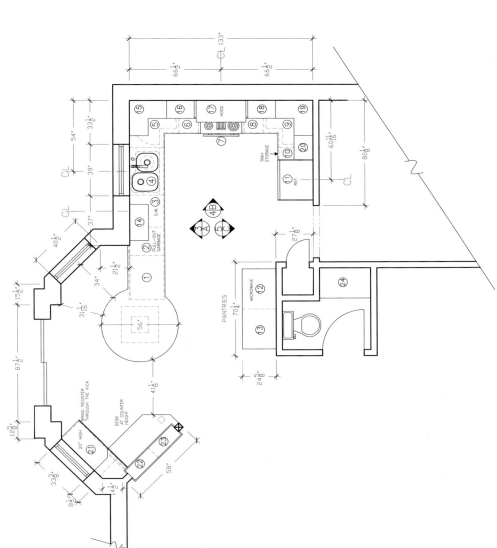

1. 33"W POTS AND PANS DRAWERS, FINISHED LEFT, FINISHED RIGHT. FINISHED PANEL ON BACKSIDE.

2. 21" PULL-OUT GARBAGE WITH 2 BINS, FINISHED RIGHT.

3. KITCHENAID DISHWASHER #KUDP02FRSS (SEE SPECS).

4. 36" SINK CABINET WITH FALSE DRAWER, FINISHED LEFT, WITH SWING-OUT COMPOST ON RIGHT DOOR. KITCHENAID BATCH FEED GARBURATOR #KBDS260X

5. 36"/36" CORNER CABINET WITH LAZY SUSAN, HINGED RIGHT.

6. 14" 4 DRAWER CABINET WITH CUTLERY DIVIDER IN TOP DRAWER, UTENSIL TRAY BELOW. 1" OVERLAY FILLER WITH PANEL TO RIGHT.

7. JENN AIR DUAL FUEL DOUBLE OVEN RANGE #JDR8895ACS

8. 14" 4 DRAWER CABINET WITH 1" OVERLAY FILLER WITH PANEL TO LEFT. CUTLERY TRAY IN TOP DRAWER, UTENSIL TRAY BELOW.

9. 36"/36" CORNER CABINET WITH LAZY SUSAN, HINGED RIGHT.

10. 9" CABINET FOR TRAYS

11. 30" LIEBHERR FRIDGE #CS1640 WITH 2 PANELS ON EITHER SIDE, AND A 30"W x 12-7/8"H x WALL CABINET ABOVE. 2-7/8" FILLER BELOW WALL CABINET.

12. 30"W X 93"H X 24-8"D TALL 3 DRAWER PANTRY CABINET WITH CENTER OPEN WITH ADJUSTABLE SHELF FOR MICROWAVE. TRAY DIVIDERS IN UPPER CABINET, FINISHED LEFT.

13. 30"W X 93"H X 24-8"D THREE DRAWER TALL PANTRY, FINISHED RIGHT, WITH SHELVING ON INSIDE DOORS IN THE MIDDLE SECTION.

14. 27" WALL CABINET, FINISHED RIGHT AND LEFT.

15. 27"/27" CORNER WALL CABINET, HINGED RIGHT, FINISHED LEFT.

16. 20" WALL CABINET, HINGED LEFT, FINISHED RIGHT.

17. 36"W X 21-7/8"H WALL CABINET WITH 36" BROAN RANGE HOOD INSTALLED BELOW. 1-1/2" OVERLAY FILLER TO RIGHT AND LEFT

18. 20" WALL CABINET, HINGED RIGHT, FINISHED LEFT.

19. 27"/27" CORNER WALL CABINET, HINGED RIGHT.

20. 18" WALL CABINET, HINGED LEFT.

21. 39"W X 17"H X 18"D BANQUETTE CABINET, INSTALLED FILLER TO LEFT.

22. & 23. WALL APOTHECARY DRAWERS, 23-3/4"W X 6"H X 10"D ON WOOD TOP. WOOD TOP OVERHANGS ON BOTH SIDES OF WALL.

24. BASE SINK CABINET FOR POWDER ROOM, 35" X 33-1/4" X 21-5/8"D. 1" FILLERS ON EITHER SIDE.

A floor plan cross-referenced to a detailed specification list ensures the cabinet quote includes everything you're expecting.

Use the following list of items and prices only as a guide.
Prices will vary depending on region.

1. Maple cabinets to a 7'-6" height, with a recessed
    panel door style in a standard stain, with
    matching crown moulding, light valance, and
    toe kick, as well as a standard accessory package
    including a cutlery tray, pull out trash bin/
    recycling bins, a few roll out shelves, one corner
    rotating shelf unit, and a couple of pot drawers: _____ $35,000

2. Mid-range granite countertops. Granite is
    priced by supply and demand. A rare species
    will cost more than a plentiful variety. Generally,
    slab is preferable to tile for a countertop.
    Counter edge thickness (single, which is ¾" or
    double, which is 1½") and profile will also affect
    the cost. This was a double square edge: _____ $8,000

3. Custom-made pedestal to match the cabinetry
    to support the counter-height table: _____ $400

4. An undermount stainless steel sink and
    chrome faucet with a pull out spray head (an
    undermount sink is one that does not have
    a metal flange sitting on top of the counter
    surface. It is literally mounted and attached to
    the underside with silicone for easier countertop
    cleaning): _____ $1,500

5. Laminate, wood-look flooring (this material
    ranges widely in price, but we used a mid-range
    variety): _____ $5,000

6. 12 Energy–efficient, compact fluorescent pot
    lights with long-lasting, color specific bulbs (I'll
    talk about lighting in more detail later): _____ $1,165

7. A decorative pendant light fixture over the table: _____ $750

8. Fluorescent under-cabinet strip lighting: _____ $600

9. Glass mosaic tile in a standard color for the
    backsplash: _____ $575

10. Cabinet knobs: _____ $200

11. Window treatments including fabric &
    drapery labor: _____ $650

12. Design fee, including project coordination &
    site supervision: _____ $4,000

13. Appliance package (mid-price & quality range): _____ $9,500

14. 6 counter height chairs: _____ $2,100

TOTAL: _____ $69,440.00

In addition to the above items, figure in labor costs for contractors who will strip out the old cabinets, flooring, appliances and plumbing fixtures, install new cabinets, flooring, backsplash, lighting, plumbing fixtures, appliances, electrical receptacles and switches, drywall (new or repair), baseboard, door and window trim, and paint. Plan on spending an additional $20,000 to $22,000 to cover these costs.

If you are handy and want to save money, you can do a lot of the work yourself, especially the demolition. But never, never cheap-out by doing the wiring or plumbing, unless you are a licensed professional. Faulty wiring can send your home up in flames. Always hire a licensed electrician, unless you are a licensed professional, whose work meets the building code requirements in your area. The same goes for plumbing; one bad connection can cause a flood that will cost you thousands more in repairs than you saved in the first place.

Other fees you'll want to plan for are delivery charges and applicable taxes. Ask for delivery charges to be billed at the end of the project. Clients often end up overpaying when charges are estimated and charged beforehand. Often, freight is determined by volume and weight, so it cannot be accurately predicted ahead of time. If you get a price beforehand, it may include a substantial mark-up to protect the cabinet dealer from getting burned on fluctuating costs. If you pay later, you both win. You may pay less and the cabinet dealer will be able to pay the shipper without fear of losing money. Just be ready for a substantial charge at the end.

Now you can clearly see how easy it is for even a modest kitchen project to add up to more than you thought possible before you began.

The considerable expense of removing a structural wall was justified by being able to add a small island to almost double the workspace of this tiny 7' x 9' kitchen. Be sure to obtain structural drawings and permits.

Condo Kitchen Before and After

Removing non-load bearing walls in this condo improved every aspect of its feel and function. Have an engineer confirm that condo walls can be moved and get a permit.

13

Designing The Kitchen

Who You Gonna Hire?

DESIGNING THE KITCHEN

Food for thought:

"Expert design advice costs a lot less than correcting mistakes made by amateurs."

- Robin Siegerman

Who You Gonna Hire?

In the world of interiors, there are several professional designations. Jurisdictions have different requirements to license or register various types of design professionals. Below is a brief overview of the qualifications and expertise you can expect from the major design disciplines. Depending on the scope of your project, one may be better suited to your needs than another.

Decorator

A decorator specializes in the aesthetics of the space. They can help pick door styles for the cabinetry, finish types, colors and materials for counters, backsplash, fabric, flooring and light fixtures. Typically they are not accredited to do the technical drawings needed by a cabinet maker, contractor, or other tradespeople to ensure a smooth renovation process. Anyone who wants to can hang out a shingle as a decorator. No experience or expertise is required. There are associations for decorators, which help to establish some practice standards, but no government agency regulates this designation.

Certified Kitchen Designer (CKD)

Typically, kitchen designers work for companies that sell cabinetry. Not all kitchen designers are certified. Some are Registered Interior Designers, but a CKD must have a combined total of seven years education and practical kitchen design experience and have passed a two-part, eight hour exam covering kitchen design and theory to test competency. In North America, the exam is administered by the NKBA (National Kitchen and Bath Association). The design portion of the exam requires the candidate to design a kitchen project using criteria given for a hypothetical client. They must conform to the 31 guidelines of kitchen design as stipulated by the NKBA professional training manuals. These guidelines cover both the safety and practicality of the kitchen layout.

The open flame of gas ranges, landing surfaces beside cook tops, ovens, and microwaves, as well as flooring surfaces and accessibility of appliances, storage, and work areas can all present a safety hazard which must be considered when designing a kitchen layout.

A CKD who works for a cabinetry seller will expect you to buy cabinets from their company once they have done the design. You may not own the drawings until you have put a deposit on the cabinets. You may choose to use an independent CKD who will sell you only the design. You then own the drawings and can "shop" them to whatever cabinet vendor you like.

Interior Designer

While the qualification process is rigorous, not all registered or licensed interior designers are experienced in kitchen design. Interior designers in most jurisdictions must be licensed or have a professional designation signifying they have passed a national two-day exam that tests competency, which in North America, is administered by the NCIDQ (National Council for Interior Design Qualifications). To be eligible to take the exam, the designer must have at least six years of practical experience in a design firm as well as an accredited design education with a minimum of a bachelor's degree or a professional diploma in interior design and a minimum of 3,520 hours of interior design work experience. The exam covers written theory which tests the professional's knowledge of building codes, standards, and construction practices and includes a practicum with a day-long drawing project. The project is based on a theoretical client with a combined commercial/residential building and a specific set of criteria. The design project must be completed by fulfilling the client's design program including interior space planning and partitions, technical drawings for plumbing, electrical, communications, and custom furniture, and all of it must meet building safety codes. Passing this exam qualifies the interior designer to practice in both commercial and residential fields.

Architectural Technologist

An Architectural Technologist with a Bachelor of Technology degree has completed four years of university-level education in architecture. Regional professional associations which govern this profession have various requirements for a professional membership designation in addition to the university degree, often including several years of internship and professional experience. In certain jurisdictions, Architectural

Technologists must pass municipal exams which will allow them to prepare permit drawings. Like architects, they may specialize in designing either new construction, restoration, or renovation of commercial or residential buildings. They may be qualified to design an addition to your home and supply you with permit drawings for construction services, but verify their experience and expertise in interior space planning, specifically kitchens, before you include the kitchen design in your contract.

Architects

Architects are design professionals who have had a minimum of six years of accredited education and 5,600 hours of internship before being eligible to take the qualifying nine-part exams. If you are contemplating removing and relocating structural walls to enlarge or relocate the kitchen, or putting on an addition, you will need to hire an architect, unless your interior designer is or has an allied professional who is licensed and/or qualified to do permit drawings. Many architects team up with an interior designer or kitchen specialist, so the interior designer or kitchen designer can create the details of the cabinet and furniture layout, materials, lighting design, and specifications based on the architectural design. Some architects prefer to do this part as well, but as with all professionals, I would advise getting references specifically from kitchen clients.

TALES FROM THE TRENCHES

One Architectural Technologist designed a house for one of my clients, and in the kitchen, he had specified a full-height refrigerator in the middle of the room with no panels or walls surrounding it. A mechanical "elephant in the room," a fridge placed with the back exposed presents a nasty view. Unless it has been carefully designed to fit into a structure that creates some kind of intentional room divider, it will create a visual obstruction and will rarely be functional. However, I work regularly with an Architectural Technologist whose practical nature and attention to detail would never lead him to commit such a no-no! Bottom line: credentials alone are no guarantee of design talent. Check references and review the portfolio of any design professional you consider bringing into your project.

When one is better than another....

A decorator is a great choice if you are redecorating your whole house, and the kitchen is just one part of the project. Your decorator is already helping you determine the overall aesthetic direction of the house and working with you to choose furniture, window treatments, carpets, and paint colors and may have a preferred kitchen designer they recommend. Generally speaking, you are well-served to go with the recommendation of someone you are already working with, like, and trust. The process of renovating is stressful and has many different components requiring specialized tradespeople to work together. If your decorator has an established team, you are much further ahead than if you have to put together a team on your own. An established team can cut down on the frequent communication breakdowns that occur when there are a dozen or more people involved. If there is a prior professional relationship, your decorator could have leverage if things start to go awry. And make no mistake, there are precious few renovations where at least one thing does not go wonky. Anyone who tells you differently is either lying or a superhero, and how many superheroes do you usually see walking around?

Don't let this confuse you, but an interior designer can also be a decorator. An interior designer can complete the technical drawings as well as help you with decisions of décor. But not all interior designers have expertise in kitchen design, so check before hiring, and talk to their references. No one is going to be silly enough to offer up an unhappy client as a reference, but if you ask the right questions, you can get the information you need to find a designer who will suit your temperament, project requirements, and budget.

Interior designers have varied compensation structures. Some have a flat fee to design the kitchen which may include lighting design and product and finish choices, but charge by the hour to help you find furniture and source fabric, and design and fabricate window treatments. Sometimes cabinet manufacturers offer professional discounts to designers, and they may be willing to share part of their savings with you. Keep in mind, a designer's expertise and working relationship with manufacturers is developed over time and is well worth compensation.

If you're considering going straight to a kitchen designer, be aware of some important points. When your design originates at a kitchen company or big box store, the mandate of the kitchen designers on staff is to get a cabinet sale. Most kitchen companies are dealers for a handful of cabinet manufacturers. Some carry a range of manufacturers from low to high-end, and some deal exclusively with custom cabinet shops. A cabinet manufacturer might be able to produce a completely custom product, but most often, they start with a specification manual of standard sizes, finishes and accessories. Using these standards wherever possible can save you money. The higher-end manufacturers are typically more amenable to building completely custom pieces, with the exception of European cabinet makers. They almost always offer modular sizes and limited finish options. They may make the Porsche of cabinets, but usually you can't customize them without paying a huge premium and enduring a lot of grumbling. Even if the manufacturer can customize, usually this option is expensive, and often the kitchen company employee will not risk losing your project by designing anything too much outside the standard manufacturer offerings. That's why it's so important to share your budget up front. The design staff will then have a better idea to what degree they can increase the complexity of the design without worrying that they are going to lose your business altogether.

In my experience, there are precious few architects who can design a functional kitchen. I know this is a controversial statement, but I just haven't met many. Kitchen design is a specialty. Just as you wouldn't go to a General Practitioner for knee surgery, an architect is not often the best choice to design your kitchen.

Years ago, when I was taking my Certified Kitchen Designer course and exam, one of my classmates was an architect. He was confident that with years of schooling, apprenticeship, and over a decade of professional experience, the kitchen design exam

TALES FROM THE TRENCHES

A few years ago, an old acquaintance from high school called saying she had seen one of my projects in a magazine and asked if she could hire me to consult on her upcoming renovation. I got there to discover she was gutting the entire house and had an architect working on the design. She wasn't sure she was getting what she asked for and wanted me to review his kitchen design. Upon first glance, I could see right away there was not enough room for the fridge door to open up 90 degrees, rendering the crisper drawers useless, as there wouldn't be room to pull them out. The architect was adamant that the contemporary design would not permit wall cabinets to visually clutter the space and ruin the purity of the design, so the walls were drawn bare, leaving no place to store dishes or food within the working area. He had provided a small walk-in pantry at one end of the room for all the storage, but the client would need to traverse the room just to get a spoon, plate, or mixing bowl. Unloading the dishwasher would have been efficient only on roller skates. Purity of line in design is great, but never at the expense of practicality.

would be a breeze. To his enormous surprise and a wee bit of humiliation, he failed the exam and had to retake it. Always remember that designing a kitchen is a specialty and more complicated than the uninitiated may assume.

How long does it take to get a kitchen design done?

At this point in the book, you may have caught on to the idea that designing a kitchen is not as simple as you may have thought at first. The design process will take some time, depending on the size of your room, your wish list, and the complexity of site conditions.

Although each designer and kitchen company works differently, in my own business, the design process consists of the following steps:

- A site measure and meeting to fill out the questionnaire (see Appendix A). (1 to 3 hours)
- Concept drawings, which are rough drawings done to scale, are more of an artistic interpretation of the client's vision. I do these before I do detailed working drawings to save time and since I'm not obsessing over every dimensional detail, it helps us solidify our direction as soon as possible. (2 to 14 days)
- A concept presentation. At this meeting, I show the concept to the client for the first time, and the client gets the opportunity to voice preferences and make changes to the design. I usually find that at this stage, a designer who has listened to the client carefully will have only minor tweaks to make to the plan. (1 to 2 hours)
- The working drawings, written legend, written scope of work. These drawings are the final "blue-print" that the tradespeople, cabinet maker, and contractor will work from. (10 to 15 days)
- The working drawing presentation is when the client reviews and signs off on the detailed drawings from which all cabinets will be ordered and work contracted. (1 to 2 hours)
- Lighting/electrical plan. This plan will not only locate the light fixtures but will specify the fixture types, bulbs, receptacle locations and voltages, light switches, cable, telephone jacks, and all the electrical requirements for the appliances. (4 to 5 days)

If everything lined up just right, this process would take a minimum three weeks from start to finish. But as most of us know, life is more convoluted, so provided you order no major changes, expect about a seven to eight week gap between having your site measured and receiving working drawings. Remember, every change you make delays the process.

Why does a three week process often take eight? Here are a few common reasons:

- The creative process is sometimes slow. If you have a complex set of requirements and some site challenges, the designer may go through a few drafts before coming up with a viable, practical, attractive design.
- Coordinating busy schedules of three or more people can take some doing. Often meetings must be scheduled well in advance, often a week out after the drawing is done. In my business, I often set the appointment before I've completely finished the concept to minimize delays.
- After the concept presentation, clients typically take a couple of days to mull over the design, discuss it with other family members, and create a list of items to address with the designer.
- The working drawings, legend, and written scope of work need to be 100% accurate. Heavily detailed, they must be cross-referenced and proofread before placing any order. For this step, the motto "go slow to go fast" applies in every case.

Just remember, you can slap together LEGO®. A masterpiece takes time.

Documentation
& Drawings

DOCUMENTATION & DRAWINGS

To embark on a renovation without drawings and documentation is foolish, a recipe for frustration, and a nightmare of never-ending upheaval. The drawings are construction documents for everyone on the job to follow to ensure the client ends up with the planned result. The people involved in a single kitchen renovation may be:

- general contractor
- drywall expert
- licensed electrician
- licensed plumber
- cabinet maker
- cabinet installer
- finish carpenter
- flooring installer
- countertop fabricator and installer
- tile setter
- painter

Imagine the chaos if all parties involved worked without a common plan.

Look at it this way: suppose you find a contractor you like. You tell him what you want to do in your kitchen. He adds a few suggestions that convince you he knows what he's talking about and says he can do the job and save you a few thousand bucks, since you don't need drawings. He explains he can just tear out the kitchen, draw an outline of the new layout on the floor and build the cabinets to suit. You get all excited, hire him and have several more conversations about the layout you want. He doesn't write anything down, and tells you to leave it to him. Are you breaking out in a cold sweat yet? I am!

If he brings in his cabinet maker and all his tradespeople to start tearing out the kitchen, the trades will be looking to him for direction for things like where all the electrical receptacles should go, where the plumbing will move to, how the flooring should be laid, where the new lighting should be placed, and what kind of trim should be going around windows and doors. He will then give them direction based on his experience and what he knows he's done on past projects. This may be fine, but it likely won't be what you have in your own head. This is where remodeling projects go sour fast, like milk left on the counter on a 100 degree day. Without a clearly documented plan, an unhappy client blames the contractor or tradespeople who "should have known better." Sorry, it's not their fault. Rather, like in the children's game of "broken telephone," if you relay a message enough times, it's bound to get lost in translation. Great party game. Bad renovation plan.

The documents you need

Even if the new kitchen layout is similar to the old one, good drawings should show and say EVERYTHING that every one of those tradespeople is going to need to know to complete the job to meet your expectations.

To prepare a kitchen design that works for you and your family, the designer will either sit down with you and ask a lot of questions, or ask you to fill out a questionnaire (See Appendix A) about how you use your kitchen (if they don't ask, you must find a way to tell them so the kitchen is designed for your habits, storage, and food preparation needs):

- How many people are in the family and what ages?
- Do any have physical disabilities?
- Does anyone in the household suffer from serious allergies or have dietary restrictions?
- How do you shop for groceries – monthly in bulk, or weekly with lots of cans and boxes?
- How much frozen food to you buy? Do you shop fresh? How often?
- Do you cook daily, a few times a week, once a week?
- What kind of cooking do you do most?

- Do you bake often?
- How many people at once are involved in the preparation of the meals?
- Are they right-handed or left-handed?
- Are there other people who use the kitchen besides you, such as a housekeeper, nanny, or caterers?
- Do you want to eat in the kitchen? How many people do you need to seat?
- What other activities take place in the kitchen, i.e. homework, games, bill paying, family scheduling?
- Do you need a desktop computer in the kitchen area or will you use a laptop? Will it be wireless?
- Do you want a TV and/or stereo in the kitchen?
- Do you have pets that need to be accommodated in the kitchen?

TAILS FROM THE TRENCHES

I had a client who kept a sizeable dog crate in the kitchen; it always seemed to be in the way and was unattractive. In the new layout, she wanted lots of working countertop space, a place for the dog crate, and also a table that could accommodate a minimum of six people for daily meals. The kitchen was sizable, but still, that was a pretty tall order. I had a brainstorm to create a large counter-height eating table attached to the island. To support the large slab of granite required, I designed a special cabinet underneath that had retractable doors with mesh inserts instead of solid panels. Inside, the client put a nice cushy dog bed, so that at night the doors were closed, and the dog was safely secured inside but could see out and had lots of air circulation. The dog loved it so much, that even during the day when the doors were open, he would scamper in there and curl up contentedly! Now THAT's a doggone good idea!

Once the designer has asked these questions and others to discover your style preferences and living habits, and after they've taken detailed measurements of the room, including window and door locations, ceiling height, and noting permanent obstructions like a soffit, a pipe chase, or a basement stairwell bulkhead, the designer is ready to come up with a drawing of your kitchen design.

As I said previously, I begin the drawing phase with a concept that is a loose interpretation of what we have discussed drawn to scale, with a few elevations to show portions of the kitchen from a front view. At this stage, I don't worry too much about precise dimensional accuracy. This is more of an artist's rendering which will help you visualize colors, materials, and style. I can prepare these concepts quickly, and for most clients, they are easier to interpret than a technical drawing. Clients are able to let me know if I'm on the right track before we commit the time to create precise drawings. If there are modifications, the new information is applied to the next stage of drawing, the working drawings.

The working drawings should include several key components:

The Plan

A bird's eye view of how the kitchen will be laid out, if there are adjoining areas like a family room, powder room, and breakfast nook – the plan should include these, so you can see how the new kitchen layout will work in relation to these spaces. Seeing your home from this view can sometimes alert you to the possibility that it may be advantageous to relocate the working kitchen into one of the adjacent areas. Or you may discover that removing the wall you planned to eliminate is not a practical option.

A plan is drawn to scale, usually one quarter inch equals one foot (1/4" = 1'-0") or one half inch equals one foot (1/2" = 1'-0") or the metric equivalent. The plan should be fully and accurately dimensioned with all physical characteristics noted, including door and window trim sizes, window and door opening sizes, permanent obstructions, and ceiling height.

Important Note! To do an accurate plan, you must choose your appliances and supply the designer with the appliance manufacturer's specifications before they do the working drawings. Without this information, you could find that the appliances don't fit when it's time to install them. Even if you think you know the sizes of the appliances, a 30" wide range might actually require 30 ¼" of clearance to install. Or a fridge that is 65" high might actually need another ¾" on top to accommodate the hinge. Failing to plan the exact amount of space required for each appliance, you are playing a very expensive game of roulette.

The plan will show the base and upper cabinets and any other features to be included like an island, peninsula, eating counter, cabinet pantry, desk, coffee bar, and baking area. Ideally, if you want any other furniture in the room like a separate dining table and chairs, or in the case of a great room, sofa and comfortable chairs, be sure these are drawn on the concept to ensure there will be enough room to accommodate your desires.

The Written Cabinet Legend

Each cabinet on the plan should be numbered and correspond to a written legend which will detail each cabinet characteristic in written form. That would include things like the size of the cabinet, whether it has drawers or doors, and what accessories are inside it, such as a cutlery tray, knife block, pull out recycling drawer, tray dividers, rotating shelves, pull out shelves, and glass inserts in the doors. Not only does this serve as the check and balance for the designer to make sure everything fits, but it provides you and the cabinet maker with a shared and clear understanding of every single detail of each cabinet. If the designer doesn't usually do a legend, ask for one. It's vital that you both understand what is going on inside each cabinet.

The Electrical Plan

Even a small kitchen benefits from having an electrical plan to indicate the number of receptacles (outlets), lighting switches, and other electrical features and **exactly** where and how high to locate them. The electrical plan also can document other features including supplementary toe kick heaters, central vac outlet, phone jacks, and TV cables. If placement is left to the contractor or electrician's discretion, you may find a thermostat in the middle of the wall where you had planned to feature a treasured piece of art. A good lighting plan uses mathematical calculations to determine which type of lighting to use and where to place it to give you optimal light for the space. You might think the one central light fixture that you've lived with for the last 20 years is adequate, but if you allow your designer to properly set the lighting, you'll wonder how you ever lived without it. Bad lighting can cause eye strain, headaches, poor focus, accidents, and feeling ill at ease in a space. I'll cover more on the specifics of lighting in a later chapter.

The Lighting & Electrical Legend

A good lighting design and electrical plan should include a legend that details each light fixture's manufacturer, the model number, and the lamp (lighting-speak for bulb) type and wattage. It should also include the types of receptacles in the kitchen (i.e. duplex = double; quad = four), their voltages (i.e. 110 for a regular receptacle; 220 for a range or a clothes dryer), and their locations. A Ground Fault Circuit Interrupter (GFCI) is indicated for a receptacle near a water source to prevent electrocution. The plan should show the symbols and explanations for types of switches and whether or not they have dimmers,

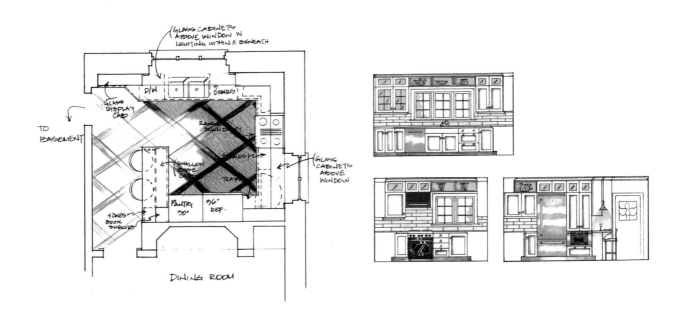

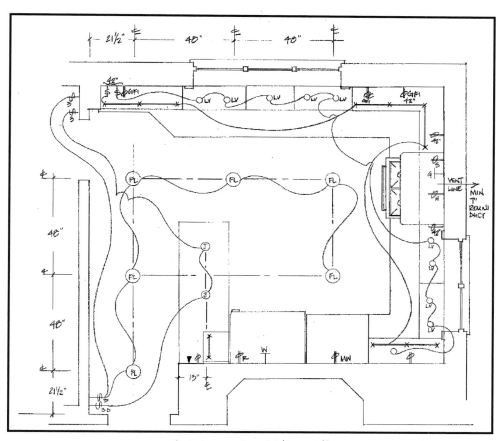

ELECTRICAL & LIGHTING LEGEND

$	SINGLE POLE LIGHT SWITCH @ 50" +/- AFF
$3D	3-WAY DIMMER SWITCH
⌀GFI 42"	GFI DUPLEX RECEPT. W/GROUND FAULT CIRCUIT INTERRUPT. @ 42" AFF
⌀C	DEDICATED GFI CIRCUIT TO BUILT IN COFFEE MAKER
⌀S	3 PRONGED 120V 15AMP RECEPT. FOR GAS VIKING RANGE
—G	GAS LINE FOR RANGE
⌀H	120 VAC, 60HZ, 6.2 AMPS CONNECTION @ 72" AFF +/-
⌀MW	120 V, 15 AMP RECEPT. FOR MICROWAVE DRAWER @ 33" +/- AFF
⌀R	FRIDGE RECEPTACLE @ 75" +/- AFF ON R SIDE FOR VIKING FRIDGE
—W	WATER LINE FOR FRIDGE
◀	PHONE JACK (CHECK HEIGHT W/CLIENT)
X—X—X	ARDEE LIGHTING XENON CLIK STRIP UNDER CAB LIGHTING 5W LAMPS
(FL)	LIGHTOLIER CALCULITE COMPACT FLUORESCENT POT LIGHTS FRAME: 4126VG120 TRIM: 8011 CCL LAMP: GE F26TBX/SPX30/4P 3000K 82CRI ←IMPORTANT
(J)	JUNCTION BOX FOR PENDANT FIXTURE CHECK W/CLIENT WHETHER 1 OR 2 REQ'D
OLV	20W RECESSED HALOGEN CABINET LIGHT UNDERNEATH OPEN SHELVES AS SHOWN, ONE PER OPEN SHELF INSIDE #100220-170 STAINLESS TRIM, THRU RICHELIEU. USE WIRE MANAGEMENT MOULDING IN WHITE #10613630 ALSO USE ONE PER CAB W/GL. DRS BUT USE 5W LAMPS

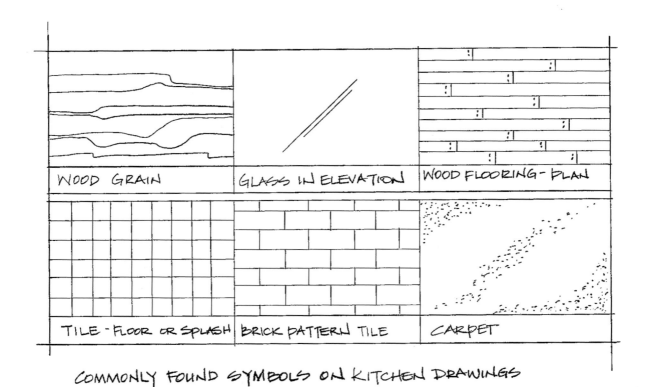

| WOOD GRAIN | GLASS IN ELEVATION | WOOD FLOORING - PLAN |
| TILE - FLOOR OR SPLASH | BRICK PATTERN TILE | CARPET |

COMMONLY FOUND SYMBOLS ON KITCHEN DRAWINGS

NORTH ARROW

BROKEN LINE BESIDE A SOLID LINE IS SHOWING A HIDDEN OBJECT LIKE A BASE CABINET UNDER A COUNTER TOP

CROSS REFERENCE SYMBOL ON A PLAN, LETTER INDICATES THE ELEVATION & NUMBER INDICATES PAGE # WHERE YOU'LL FIND IT.

BROKEN LINE ON ITS OWN INDICATES A WALL OR OBJECT TO BE DEMOLISHED

RECTANGLE WITH CLOSELY SPACED, PARALELL LINES INDICATES A NEW STUD WALL or if lights are operated from more than one location (commonly referred to as a 3-way or higher). Cable and phone outlets and hardwiring (an electrical connection that needs no plug on the end) for things like a vent hood or dishwasher all should be labeled on the legend.

The Elevation

The plan should include symbols which tell you on what page and where on the page you can find the front view of a particular wall of cabinets. The arrows should point to the walls that will be shown in elevation. The page and drawing number are located inside the symbols. They should look something like the illustration on the right.

CROSS REFERENCE SYMBOL ON A PLAN. LETTER INDICATES THE ELEVATION & NUMBER INDICATES PAGE # WHERE YOU'LL FIND IT.

An elevation is a two-dimensional drawing, meaning it gives you a flat view as though you were standing in front of a wall of cabinets. So for example, you can see where the display cabinets will be located in relation to the window, or where the pot drawers will be in relation to the appliances.

In kitchen design specifically, elevations show you the width and height of each cabinet at both the base and on the wall. The conventional home has 8'-0" high ceilings and 36" high countertops; typically, the space between the countertop and the underside of the wall cabinets is 18", and the wall cabinets may be 30" (two and a half feet high), 36", or 39" high, depending on how close to the ceiling you want to go and whether or not you need to account for crown moulding. (If you are not planning on crown moulding but want the cabinets to go flush to the ceiling, I advise you to have a small panel matching the cabinet finish between the top of the cabinets and the ceiling. If the ceiling is not level and you try to install your cabinets tight to the ceiling, you may not be able to open the doors.)

The Scope of Work

Many kitchen designers don't prepare this document, but I find it invaluable to itemize the work that is to be done that may not show up on the drawings or legend, particularly for complex projects. This way no one forgets to do anything (unless they don't read it). I use this document when getting quotes from contractors, so they are all bidding based on the same information. After all, there is little point in comparing apples with kumquats.

The scope of work is broken down into sections:

1. Expectations on the job site
2. Areas to be demolished
3. Areas to be rebuilt or refinished

The expectations on the job site can include things such as:

- No smoking inside the house
- No cigarette butts thrown outside
- All food containers must be disposed of daily and not left on-site (imagine a half-finished coffee getting knocked over onto the newly-laid floor)
- Existing flooring that is not being replaced must be covered with masonite to protect it during construction
- All re-useable items such as cabinets, countertop, sink, faucet, and decorative lighting which will not be incorporated into the new kitchen should be taken to Habitat for Humanity Re-Store for recycling and reuse
- The job site must be tidied and swept at the end of each work day.

Areas to be demolished could read something like this:

- All cabinets, countertops, under cabinet lighting, sinks and faucets are to be carefully removed for recycling. Built-in hutch to remain.
- Non-structural wall between kitchen and eating area to be removed (see plan and elevation 1/B).

TALES FROM THE TRENCHES

One past client of mine who lived in a century home wanted her cabinet crown moulding to go tight to the ceiling. We discovered that not only was the ceiling not level, the floor was not level and the walls were not plumb (straight up and down). There was a 3" difference from one side of the room to the other. With these conditions, I would normally not recommend that the crown moulding touch the ceiling, for it will be tight up against it in some places with a large gap in others, but she was adamant, no space between the crown and the ceiling. We had to use a firring strip (a panel matching the cabinets) from the top of the cabinets to the ceiling, scribing (cutting the top edge to match the undulation of the ceiling) the top, then mounting the crown on top of that to get it as tight to the ceiling as possible. Because most crown moulding is wood, there is only so far you can bend it, and if the ceiling is way out as in this case, there will still be some gaps. To please the client, the installer cut slivers of matching cabinet material and used them to fill the space gaps. I then called in the cabinet refinisher who filled and touched up the seams and gaps with matching stain. The result was beautiful, but it was very labor intensive and expensive.

- Existing flooring in working area to be removed, floor in family room and adjacent hall to remain (see plan).
- All window and door trim and baseboards to be removed and recycled, if possible.
- Wallpaper in adjoining family room to be stripped.
- Soffit in kitchen cabinet area to be demolished.

Areas to be rebuilt or refinished could read something like this:
- Wall between kitchen and eating area to be rebuilt as 42" high knee wall with glass insert (see elevation 1/B and section 2/B). Note: a section is a drawing that shows a slice of something as though you had taken a knife and cut through it. This will answer a contractor's questions about how something is to be put together. It can also be used to show specialty mouldings or cabinets.
- Recessed lighting (also called pot lights or cans) and switches to be located as per lighting plan.
- Plumbing to be relocated as per plan. Note: dimensions on the plan should show the plumber exactly where to rough in the pipes for the new sink location, and if required, water line to the fridge, built-in ice maker, and/or bar sink.
- Flooring to be laid prior to cabinet installation as per pattern shown on plan.
- Window and door trim # 23 from XYZ Millwork Supplier to be primed and installed.
- Baseboard #32 from XYZ Millwork Supplier to be primed and installed after cabinetry.
- All walls and ceiling to be dry-walled, sanded, and made ready for painting.
- Walls to be painted prior to cabinet installation with touch up after, as required.
- Cabinet supply and installation by others. Note: this applies if you're using a kitchen company who is not in the employ of the contractor.
- Countertop installation by others.
- Backsplash tile to be installed as per pattern shown in elevation 1/B AFTER countertop installation.

If all of this seems like a huge amount of information, it is, but imagine not having it all written down, so everyone knows what they're supposed to do when they show up for work on your home. Skip this step at your peril!

Now let's move on to some pretty stuff.

Deciding on Style

DECIDING ON STYLE

Before we go into style, I first want to debunk a popular myth about "timeless style." There is no such thing as a timeless style. I know, I know…every magazine and designer talks about "timeless style," but everything goes out of style eventually, and eventually, every design looks dated. Some styles will have a longer life than others, and some trendy styles will be in and out in a flash. Trendy styles are typically contemporary, with unusual color combinations or materials. But even kitchens like these will work for you if that's what you love.

On average, a style has a life span of about 10 to 15 years. After that, the kitchen will look dated and shabby, and the buyer will want to re-do it anyway. If you're picking a style to sell your house, you'd better plan to move within three years, so it still looks new and current.

Sometimes the style of the kitchen is dictated by the architecture of the house. If you own a historical Victorian home with authentic architectural details like ceiling medallions, hefty cornice mouldings, decorative gingerbread (usually curly wooden bracket-type details), and original stained glass windows, to put in a super glossy, contemporary kitchen would detract from the beauty of the home. It won't sit comfortably within the bones of the house.

In my mind, there are a few scenarios where a contemporary kitchen works well:

- In an old house that has been gutted inside and the whole remodeled interior has a consistently contemporary style.

- A house with no historical significance and no strong architectural style of its own, so you can make it anything you want.

- A brand new house that has been built in the modernist style (you'll recognize it instantly because it often lacks historical reference points like a pitched roof, front porch, and it is usually very square and lacks embellishments).

But ultimately, it's your house; you are going to have to live there and you need to feel comfortable in it, and if you're not going to be trying to sell in the next few years, you are best served to create a kitchen in whichever style will make you happy.

Just remember, no matter which style you prefer, function must always be the first consideration.

Traditional

Traditional style doesn't only have to look like it belongs in a baronial castle like you may see in the ads of glossy décor magazines. In fact in most houses, a kitchen with details befitting a castle would look strange and out of place. More common traditional elements include detailed door styles with raised panels, elaborately carved mouldings, corbels, pilasters and legs, as well as ornate, carved appliqués on panels and cabinet-match panels on

A new kitchen in the Victorian style lives in an authentic Victorian row house.

36

appliance doors. When used in moderation, some of these details can be elegant, but if overused they create a distinctly garish, "nouveau riche" look. Traditional style can encompass a wide variety of interpretations from French Provincial, Tuscan, American Country, and Arts and Crafts to English Country, with many variations of each and many not even mentioned. Let your designer guide you to make the most stylish choices. Keep in mind, each era reinterprets the style, so a traditional kitchen in the twenty-first century will look nothing like the same style did in the 1970s.

Transitional

Transitional style can be interpreted in different ways, but most often it is a cross between traditional and contemporary. Typically, it has less fussy detail than a traditional kitchen, but more detail than a contemporary kitchen.

A transitional kitchen style may have cabinet doors with a recessed center panel instead of a raised panel and simple mouldings with nary a carved corbel in sight. Transitional may also incorporate elements of other cultures such as China or Japan in a muted, stylized way, or other eras such as the Mission Style from the early twentieth century.

Transitional style is quite easy to live with since you can emphasize its contemporary nature with companion furnishings, but traditional furnishings will be equally at home in that setting.

Transitional style has a mix of both contemporary and traditional elements.

Contemporary

Contemporary often gets a bad rap as cold and unwelcoming, but this is not necessarily so. Contemporary style, as it is interpreted today, has clean lines, almost no adornment of any kind and no mouldings; however, using color and texture can keep contemporary kitchens from looking sterile.

Contemporary designs usually feature stainless steel appliances. Sometimes stainless steel countertops and decorative hardware punctuate the design. Adding some natural or stained wood with contrasting colors will add warmth.

The most common door style in contemporary kitchens is a slab door, or one that is flat, but maybe has edges with a soft radius. A Shaker style door, which has a perfectly square frame around a recessed panel with square edges also can be used in a contemporary kitchen, but it is equally suitable for a transitional style room.

Contemporary kitchen with slab doors in a glossy, wood grain laminate. Durable and beautiful.

NOTE: If a slab door is wood, it is typically veneer, a paper-thin layer of the actual species of wood laminated to a core of more stable material like medium density fiber board. This is less likely to warp, shrink or twist than a solid piece of wood.

Wood is a living, breathing material and, even after it has been cut and finished, it absorbs moisture from the surrounding atmosphere that can cause swelling. If the air is too dry, the atmosphere will suck the moisture out of the wood, causing it to shrink. A veneer over a core of material like particle board or medium density fibreboard (MDF), will stay stable through the changing atmospheric conditions.

Veneer does not mean your cabinet doors are "cheap." On the contrary, it means they are well-made. For the same reason, a flat, recessed panel in the center of a cabinet door may also be a veneer panel. This is particularly advisable with a dark stained wood, so the center panel will not shrink in dry weather, exposing an unfinished stripe of wood around the perimeter of the panel. Interior heating systems are particularly hard on wood products. To make sure your wood furniture doesn't split, crack, or warp, you should have some means of humidifying the interior. On the flip side, in tropical climates, try to have a system that extracts excess humidity from the air.

When I moved into my current home, it was a mish-mash of styles. Built in 1937, the rooms were laid out in a traditional pattern. In a 1970s bid to modernize the interior, the previous owner removed the traditional wood handrail and pickets from the central staircase and created a half-wall topped with a wide slab of blonde oak, sprayed the hallways with stucco, and installed a contemporary kitchen, covered floor to ceiling in white laminate and accented with mud-brown ceramic floor tiles. In the dining and living rooms, the traditional features remained. The house looked fragmented and felt awkward. Conclusion: only radically change the style of the kitchen if you have the means to update the rest of the house to match. If your budget only covers the kitchen, choose a style that compliments the rest of the house. This is when a Transitional Style will rescue you from a bad style mistake.

TALES FROM THE TRENCHES

Modern

Modernist kitchens are the ones that look most austere, relative to the preferences of the general population in North America. Although the cabinets may be made from natural wood, the layout is often unconventional in the sense that there may be fewer wall cabinets, or there may be a whole wall of floor to ceiling cabinets with the only working countertop on a central island. Sometimes these kitchens are monochromatic, with no contrasting color to give it visual punch. Some people find this soothing, while others feel physically chilly when considering this style.

From the standpoint of design, it is creative and challenging to design kitchens in various styles, rather than designing with one style over and over again. As long as it is safe, functional, practical, and reflects the taste of the owner, it will work. If the room is an adequate size, and there is not enough storage space for practical use, I don't care how beautiful it is, that kitchen is a flop.

Baulthaup

Very modern styles can be visually striking but are usually minimalist in nature like these

Before and After

Re-orienting the island improved the traffic flow and work space.

Picking Cabinets,
Materials & Colors

CHAPTER 5

PICKING CABINETS, MATERIALS & COLORS

Food for thought:

"A do-it-yourselfer walked into a lumberyard and asked the clerk if they carried 2x4's. The clerk nodded and asked how long he wanted them. The customer responded, "Well, I guess for about 20 years, I'm remodeling my kitchen. "

- Unknown

When picking materials and colors, *don't be afraid!!*

Did I just hear you say, "That's ridiculous, Robin! I'm not afraid of color!"? If so, I applaud you! Many people I talk to about redoing their kitchen are afraid of color, even if they don't recognize their aversion as fear. When we start talking color, body language shifts…the client may sit back in their chair, cross their arms, tense their shoulders….they don't recognize their apprehension, even though their language often reveals their concern. The client may say things like, "I'm *afraid* I'll get tired of it" or "I'm *afraid* my house won't sell." Well, like I've said several times already, if you think you're going to have to or want to sell your house in the next two to three years, by all means do something neutral that will be as inoffensive as possible and will appeal to the largest number of prospects. But if you're going to live in your house for the next 10 to 15 years, surround yourself with colors that make you feel good and don't listen to your mother/brother/sister/aunt/cousin/neighbor/friend, unless they're paying for it and are living there with you. Everyone you ask will profess to be an expert and have an opinion about what you should or shouldn't do, whether or not they have any experience. By the time you're done polling everyone you know, you'll be in a hopeless muddle and paralyzed with indecision. If you're working with a designer (and I hope by this time you won't consider attempting this project without one), trust their instincts. They are trained professionals and finding color combinations you like is part of their range of services. Be sure you *do* consult your mate/partner/husband/wife, because one of the objectives of this book is that you have a successful remodel *and* keep your spouse.

Once you've overcome your fear of color, be sure you keep your commitment to being practical. For example, if your kitchen has little natural light, and your budget does not allow for a lighting overhaul, dark colors and matte finishes will absorb what little light there is and the room will appear dim and gloomy. In contrast, light colors and glossy finishes will reflect the available light, brightening the room. If you have a bunch of kids and a menagerie of pets, pick finishes that will stand up to wear, clean up easily, and won't look grubby. There's no point in clipping a magazine photo of a pristine, white kitchen, with white marble countertops, stainless steel appliances, and pale stone floors. Spills, footprints, pet hair, and fingerprints will rule your world. Maybe you can do that in your next life, or when the kids grow up and move out and you live alone with a white cat. Balance preference with practicality or you'll be unhappy in short order.

> **NOTE:** If your kitchen cabinets are painted wood, be aware that anywhere there is a joint, when the wood expands and contracts, you will see a hairline crack, unless the components are veneer and you're using a medium to dark color. This is not a defect! Wood is a living, breathing material and naturally expands and contracts with shifts in temperature and humidity. Unless the humidity and temperature are rigidly controlled, the wood will shrink in Northern climates, causing a hairline separation of the joints, which causes a shadow line which looks like a crack in a painted finish. In my view, this is desirable, as it tells me that the cabinets are real wood and not made of plastic or some other synthetic.

Natural materials

Natural materials like wood, stone, bamboo, and cork, can provide wonderful warm additions to the kitchen, yet even apart from environmental impact they have both advantages and disadvantages.

Disadvantages may include:
- Unpredictable color variations and graining
- Can develop a worn look over time and may require re-finishing to restore its original lustre
- If the wood is a veneer, great care must be taken if refinishing or you may wear away the wood itself in your quest to remove only the finish. Before you start, consult a refinishing expert!

Some of the disadvantages listed above can also be considered advantages, such as the unpredictable color variations and graining of wood. This gives the material a natural, unique personality. Synthetic materials can sometimes appear too regular to be attractive and may take on a "fake" look, depending on the quality or what look you are trying to achieve. This is also subjective and varies according to your taste.

Contemporary but warm, the veneer cabinets benefit from the contrast of the black Paperstone counter top

Synthetic or man-made materials

Synthetic materials can be visually more consistent than natural materials, but can possibly present a health hazard from off-gassing. Off-gassing is the toxic vapor emitted by some synthetic materials into a home's atmosphere, sometimes long after a product has been installed. Off-gassing can also occur when natural materials have a synthetic finish. These toxic fumes are known as VOCs or volatile organic compounds. These VOCs can cause a variety of health problems. If you or someone in your family has allergies, be sure to carefully research materials and finishes to reduce the potential health hazards as much as possible.

Man-made products can sometimes try to incorporate a modest variation of color and pattern to more closely resemble a natural product such as wood-look laminate flooring, or porcelain tiles with a veined pattern meant to resemble stone. Some man-made products may actually have natural ingredients mixed in which are then manipulated or altered in some way so the characteristics are more predictable. An example of this is some quartz countertops are composites of real stone particulates, synthetic binders, and pigments. There are several brands on the market each with their own characteristics and varying degrees of natural material. One such brand, Zodiaq® by Dupont, claims 93% quartz content.[1] It is available in an array of colors, with many neutrals to resemble natural materials. A competing product, Silestone®,[2] incorporates an antimicrobial component which inhibits mold, mildew, and the proliferation of bacteria, which is a terrific advantage in food preparation areas. This product also has a Greenguard® certification for indoor air quality, which means its chemical emissions are lower than others on the market.

Specifics of materials

Cabinets

Wood: Common species for cabinets and doors are oak, maple, cherry, pine, ash, walnut, alder, and recently, bamboo. Less common are more exotic species such as Bird's Eye maple (the "eyes" are actually caused by a disease in the tree), wenge, rosewood, zebra wood, mahogany, purple heart, lyptus, beech, anegre, apple, olive, padauk, and bubinga.[3] Wood can be finished with stain, paint, clear varnish, oil, or wax. Exotics are most often only given a clear coat to enhance the wood's natural hue. Domestic species are often stained to even out the color variations within planks and sheets of veneer. Most cabinet boxes are a particle board or plywood core with a melamine, vinyl, or wood veneer interior finish.

When using wood for cabinets instead of a man-made material like laminate, consider the advantages:
- Distinctive characteristics and color variations in the wood and graining give it a

[1] Dupont™ Global Website. (2008) http://www2.dupont.com/Zodiaq/en_GB/index.html, [2] Silestone® (2007) www.silestoneusa.com, [3] Hobbit House (2008). Retrieved January 3, 2009 www.hobbithouseinc.com

unique personality and authenticity, which as previously discussed may be seen as a disadvantage by some people

- Wood is recyclable
- Can develop a patina over time, giving it a weathered appeal and sometimes can be refinished, but again, can be turned into a negative depending on your perspective
- Depending on the wood, it can be finished in a variety of ways as discussed above

Wood-Mode

Slab doors are most often found in a modern or contemporary style kitchen

MDF: (medium density fibreboard): This is the material most commonly used for lacquered doors and panels. Particle board or plywood is most often used for cabinet boxes with MDF end panels finished in the matching door lacquer. MDF is a type of very dense hardboard which is made from wood fibre glued under heat and pressure[4] and is used for cabinet doors when a lacquer finish requires a perfectly smooth surface. It has no grain and is ideal for high-gloss lacquer finishes. A high-gloss lacquer on wood will highlight any bumpy texture beneath the finish and mar the velvety texture. A lacquer is a sprayed-on finish that can either be matte or glossy and should be perfectly smooth. A rough feel when you run your hand over it means there is overspray, where a second coat has overlapped the first coat spoiling the smooth surface.

Laminate: Sometimes known by one of its brand names such as Formica®, laminate is made from many thin layers of craft paper pressed together under pressure and heat with a thin layer of patterned or colored paper on top then sealed with a clear plastic layer. Laminate is used to cover a core of particle board for cabinet boxes, doors, and even countertops.

Merit Kitchens

The deeper color of the cherry floor provides a warm contrast to the natural maple cabinetry

Stainless steel: When used on cabinet doors and drawer fronts, there is usually a core of particle board wrapped with a thin sheet of stainless steel either front and back, or just on the front with a laminate on the back for a less costly version.

Glass doors: These can be either frameless or, more commonly, as an insert in a wood, stainless, or aluminum frame. The glass itself can be clear textured, frosted, seeded, or colored as in stained glass.

Orange is a great color but should be used with care. Too much in the wrong places in the wrong shade can be garish.

Before

After

Robin Stubbert

48

The price of cabinetry is also affected by whether the cabinets are framed or frameless construction. Framed means you can see the face frame of the box around the perimeter of the door, whether the door sits on top of the frame or is flush with the frame, known as an inset door. In these applications, the hinges are usually visible, whereas with a frameless door, the hinges are completely hidden and the frame of the box is completely covered by the door. Framed is more expensive, as it requires more material and labor to construct.

Countertops

With a huge number of countertop material choices available, the best choice for you will be determined by your budget, your willingness to maintain it, and your slob quotient (that's my own technical term).

Whether natural or synthetic, beware of a high-gloss finish on materials with little or no pattern. The glossy finish will show things like dried water spots, scratches, crumbs, and finger prints. A matte (honed) finish on stone can give it a softer, aged look but some stone then loses its visual depth and vibrancy. In this case, you can apply a sealant with a color-enhancer to bring out the natural depth of color, but even so, some stone has a dead look without a glossy finish. If natural stone counter tops are not sealed, their porous nature will leave the material vulnerable to staining

A counter top in honed black granite looks beautiful but will show every water spot and crumb.

and etching. Etching occurs when an acidic compound, like a citrus juice, vinegar, or wine removes the gloss from the surface. Foods with strong colors such as red wine, blueberries, strawberries, beets, mustard, and curry can cause staining. Sometimes using a poultice of baking soda and water on the stain can help to make it less obvious, but to remove it completely, the countertop will have to be professionally refinished and even then, some stains are permanent.

Marble: Natural stone distinguished by undulating veins of a contrasting color to the background. Highly porous, marble should always be sealed, can have a polished or honed finish, and can develop an attractive patina of wear over time.

Granite: Very commonly used for countertops due to its density and resistance to staining, granite comes in many patterns and colors, but it is often identifiable by particulates of contrasting minerals, with little or no veining and can be polished or honed. Recent concerns about some granite emitting toxic radiation indicate that you may want to have your granite tested by a mitigation technician.[5]

Soapstone: Often free of veining or color variations, soapstone is a preferred choice for those wanting a clean but natural look. However, it is a soft stone, so can be prone to fissures and cracks. It must be oiled regularly to maintain its lustre.

Plastic Laminate: A very economical choice available in hundreds of colors, patterns, and textures, plastic laminate is only modestly durable. It's vulnerable to burns, scratching, chipping, and staining. If it has been poorly made, the seams may be vulnerable to water penetration, swelling the particle board beneath and giving the top an ugly, permanent bulge.

Solid surface materials: Popular brand names such as Corian®, Gibralter®, and Avonite are non-porous, man-made materials. Most solid surface materials can allow slabs to be joined together with a practically invisible seam.

TALES FROM THE TRENCHES

When I first used cork as flooring in my kitchen back in 1992, no one seemed to know much about it. There were very few suppliers in my area that carried it, and the color choices were the natural variations of brown, brown, and brown. Being a designer, and determined to use my own house as my laboratory, I was adamant that I wanted my cork floor to be red. Yup. Cranberry, to be precise. No one could tell me how to achieve this color, so I devised a tinted polyurethane. As it turns out, I loved the cork! But after a few years with kids and dogs skidding around the kitchen, my improvised finish eventually started to show unattractive signs of wear. Ten years later in my next house, I was determined to again have a red cork floor, but by then, manufacturers were answering the call for durable, colored materials. The cork is just as wonderful a material as it was then, but now, almost 10 years later still with kids and dogs thundering through the kitchen, the color remains strong and true, a shining example of a natural material with a synthetic finish successfully applied to enhance its appeal and durability.

[5] *New York Times.* July 2008. Kate Murphy. http://www.nytimes.com/2008/07/24/garden/24granite.html?_r=3&oref=slogin

Darker colors tend to show scratches more than lighter colors, but they can sometimes be buffed out if they don't go too deep. Most slabs are 3/4" thick and the color is consistent all the way through.

Quartz: This is a man-made stone slab, using up to 93% natural stone, polymer binders, pigments, and sometimes recycled material such as colored glass and mirror. It comes in many colors but patterns are mostly composed of particulates. Most commonly available with a glossy finish, quartz is durable, resists staining, scratching, and burning, and is low maintenance. Some brands available are Zodiaq®, Silestone®, Caesarstone®, Cambria®, and HanStone®. Silestone's anti-microbial treatment does not wear off. It is impregnated into the slabs.

Wood: These countertops can be beautiful but are often high maintenance, depending on the wood and construction methods. Teak wood, which is often used on boats and outdoor furniture, works well around a water source, but must be oiled frequently with mineral oil (available at pharmacies). Scratches can be

Ted Yarwood

Be prepared to keep a wood counter top regularly oiled with butcher block oil or mineral oil. Like skin, raw wood will dry out and crack if not maintained

sanded out with a fine grit sandpaper followed by an oil treatment. Unless wood tops are constructed properly, they will be subject to terrible warping and splitting. Not a recommended DIY project.

Glass: These tops can be an excellent feature piece and if used well, visually striking with artistic options like backlighting and custom colored designs. I don't recommend clear glass for your main prep area, as it scratches easily. A textured underside and colored designs can help hide scratches and fingerprints. For a contemporary interior, glass has a real wow factor and is non-porous, so it's sanitary and can be recycled.

Concrete: This material is usually used in contemporary installations. Although it is man-made, concrete is fabricated with natural substances and can be pigmented and decorated with inlays of various contrasting materials for added visual interest. Concrete should be sealed periodically to maintain its stain resistance. Usually poured into forms and installed on top of the cabinets in slabs, a well-made concrete top can be beautiful looking, but if it's improperly fabricated it can be subject to cracking and chipping, so it must be made by someone very experienced in working with the material. Geocrete, developed by the renowned architect Fu-Tung Cheng, is a concrete formula that is made by certified fabricators and has been used to stunning effect.

Geocrete, Cheng Design

A concrete top can be customized with inlayed items like shells, metal, and glass

Paperstone

Paperstone™ countertops are a green alternative

Slate: This stone has a slow absorption rate, so it's naturally stain resistant. It naturally occurs with a matte appearance, and it can be rubbed with oil to add lustre. Use an oil that is safe for food preparation areas like mineral oil, since it won't go rancid like food-based oils. A chemical sealer will also add sheen.

Paperstone™: This is a newer addition to the countertop market. It is made from 100% post-consumer recycled paper and a non-petroleum phenolic resin derived in part from natural phenolic oil found in the shells of cashews. It is certified by the Smartwood program of the Rainforest Alliance to FSC standards, so is classified as a truly "green" product.[6]

Icestone®: This man-made material is made from 100% recycled glass and cement to make a highly durable, beautiful concrete surface in a variety of colors that have a luminous sparkle. It is also considered a green material with no VOCs.[7]

Metal: These countertops can be stainless steel, which in the higher grades is extremely sanitary and resists staining, but it scratches easily. Copper develops a patina of verdigris (green oxidization) unless coated with a protective finish, so it's best not to use for food preparation areas. Zinc has a softer lustre than stainless steel and over time will oxidize down to a dark grey color which beautifully compliments antique woods and finishes; however, it is costly.

Backsplash

The backsplash is the area between the countertop and the underside of the wall cabinets. Although it does not suffer from the same wear and tear as a countertop or cabinet, as its name suggests, it is often splashed by innumerable substances. The best backsplash is easy to wipe down and clean. Because of its relatively small area requiring less product, it's also a great spot to splurge on more expensive materials to upgrade the overall look of an otherwise modest kitchen.

Tile is the most common form of backsplash material whether it is made of stone, ceramic, porcelain, or glass.

A high-end custom made stainless steel counter top can have a seamlessly integrated sink

Stone slabs to match or contrast the countertop are easily cleaned, especially since it has the advantage of very few seams and no grout lines for grime to collect in.

Glass can either be used in tile or sheet form, comes in a wide variety of delicious colors, and can be matte or glossy, which gives the backsplash area visual depth and sparkle. Sheets of glass can be custom back-painted so the color is protected from cleaning products. Sheet glass can be difficult to cut precisely and must be tempered, so it may not tightly meet the ceiling line if it is going all the way from counter surface upward. These gaps will usually be filled with clear silicone.

Laminate is a huge money saver and comes in interesting patterns, textures, and colors, so can create a dynamic look if it covers the entire backsplash. However, seams are difficult to camouflage or join inconspicuously. Sometimes a laminate backsplash is part of the countertop and only 3" to 6" high, leaving the rest of the space free to be covered with paint or wallpaper. This is a budget conscious treatment and in my opinion, one of the least attractive options.

Visual emphasis is placed on this tile backsplash by using wide grout lines in a contrasting color

Brent Foster

A stone slab with dramatic pattern can be a dynamic backsplash

Painted wall board is the least expensive and least practical option. If you have a bad spill on the counter, unless it is wiped up immediately before it hits the back wall, you may experience some wall damage. Once wall board is saturated with moisture, mold is sure to grow. If you are not planning a protective backsplash material that is impervious to water, you should at least use cement board, which will not grow mold if it gets wet.

Flooring

There are a dizzying array of flooring choices available, and some will be more practical for your personal situation than others. When considering the options, ensure you know the durability and maintenance required so you can make the most appropriate choice.

Stone tile is a popular option but should come with a huge warning sign: don't make the colossal mistake of looking at one or two square feet of natural stone (or any natural product for that matter) and assume that a room full of it will look entirely uniform. As previously discussed, the wonderful thing about natural materials is their variation in color, pattern, and texture. You have to be willing to accept some uncertainty, otherwise you'll be safer with man-made materials. Natural stone should be sealed regularly to prevent staining.

Wood flooring is an increasingly popular option in kitchens. It looks beautiful and warm, but if you have high traffic volume or are careless about maintenance, it can look shabby and worn after just a few years. Dark stains show damage more quickly than light ones.

Ceramic or porcelain tile can be a very economical choice and it's practical, but as with any kind of tile, beware of the grout. Even if it is sealed, grout with a light color begins to look grubby in the main traffic areas soon after installation even if sealed. Better to use a medium dark colored grout to minimize the appearance of grunge. Tile floors are unforgiving when things are dropped on them and can be cold and uncomfortable to stand on for long periods of time if you have any physical challenges like knee, hip or back problems.

Bamboo has surged in popularity in recent years for those who want the look of wood with a slight twist. Quick regeneration makes this an environmentally responsible choice (typically, an oak tree must grow for 80 years before it is harvested for its wood), needing three to six years before harvesting. Depending on how it is cut, the planks may obviously show the knuckles of the bamboo stalks. Typically, bamboo is harder than hardwoods commonly used in flooring and works best if it is left close to its natural color rather than stained dark.

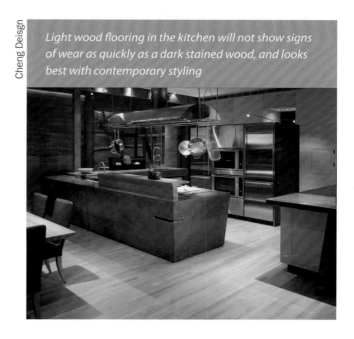

Cheng Deisgn

Light wood flooring in the kitchen will not show signs of wear as quickly as a dark stained wood, and looks best with contemporary styling

Contrasting colored grout will emphasize a tile pattern.

A combination of flooring materials can create interesting patterns like this terracotta tile floor with antique weathered wood accents.

Glass tile on a backsplash can add vibrant sparkle or muted translucency depending on the finished used. The floor is also tempered glass tile.

Cork has an interesting natural pattern, is resilient, warm underfoot, and has a soft sound. It is also very forgiving when something is dropped on it. It is available as a 1/4" thick tile which is glued down directly to the sub floor, or as a "floating floor" which is a tongue and groove system that clicks together in planks but is not attached to the sub floor. Like bamboo, it's an environmentally sound choice. It is taken from the bark of a cork oak which regenerates in an average of nine years. With a factory-applied finish it comes in other colors besides bulletin-board brown and each piece is unique giving it visual interest.

Linoleum has come a long way from the material that was popular in my grandmother's day and comes in many more colors than just the hospital green or grey of years past. It's soft, resilient, and is easily maintained, comes in either a sheet or tile, and can be cut and inlaid in interesting ways to create eye-popping designs. The color goes all the way through the material so scratches are not easily seen. It is made up of a variety of natural components including linseed oil, wood or cork flour, burlap, canvas, or hemp with various pigments.

Laminate flooring can be a practical option in a kitchen where you want the look of wood but need a more durable material. As with other materials, there are many grades, some of which have a plastic sound when you walk on them with hard-soled shoes. High-grade laminate flooring will be constructed so it will not warp or twist and will have a cork backing to dull the hollow sound.

Vinyl comes in sheets or tiles and is relatively inexpensive when compared to natural wood or stone. Unlike linoleum, it has only a thin layer of color on the top, so scratches may show up as black. Moderately durable and extremely low maintenance, it comes in a wide array of colors and patterns. Although not an environmentally friendly choice, some manufacturers do use recycled vinyl content. Be very careful with any resilient flooring material: if the sub floor is not perfectly smooth, the seams and bumps will show through the flooring shortly after installation. Also, if it is being installed in an older home and the floor settles causing the sub floor to shift, this will also show through the material.

Robin Stubbert Photography

Marmoleum flooring can be used with different colors and patterns to create a custom design

Lighting

Food for thought:

How many contractors does it take to screw in a light bulb?

They're very busy right now. They'll try to get a quote to you in a week or so...

CHAPTER 6

LIGHTING

Poor kitchen lighting is one of my pet peeves. It can cause eye strain, headaches, general malaise, and can set the stage for a nasty accident. However, lighting preferences are completely subjective. I am always amazed when I go into someone's home and they prefer working in an atmosphere with lighting that I consider funereal.

A well-planned lighting design will provide a few different layers of light combining general lighting, task lighting, decorative lighting, and accent lighting which can be used simultaneously or independently and regulated with dimmers to set various tones and moods. As we age, visual acuity decreases which means our need for concentrated, glare-free task lighting increases. Since the only person who ever seemed to age backwards was Brad Pitt's Benjamin Button movie character, we all must prepare ourselves and our interiors, so we don't get lost in the dark.

Quality efficient lighting in the kitchen is neither a solitary ceiling-mounted light fixture in the center of the room nor is it a bunch of pot lights placed at regular intervals in the ceiling and connected to a dimmer switch. A comprehensive lighting plan uses mathematical calculations to determine the lighting requirements, allowing you to buy the right stuff and put it in the right place.

Lighting design is as close to actual rocket science as you're going to get in this book. Here are some of the considerations that go into calculating optimal light levels in the kitchen.

Light colored vertical surfaces at eye level will reflect light back into the room, so the room requires fewer light fixtures to achieve optimal light levels

Robin Stubbert Photography

Surface colors and calculations

Color both reflects and absorbs light. If a light color reflects 50% of the light that hits it, that means it is also absorbing the other 50%. A dark color will absorb more light than it reflects, but the actual reflectance percentages depend on the value or darkness of the dark color (i.e. light brown vs. dark brown). If your ceiling, cabinets, countertops, and flooring were all dark brown (which means you're either a bachelor vampire or you haven't consulted a color expert), you'd need a pile more light fixtures with brighter lamps than you would to get the same light levels if all those same surfaces were pale yellow.

Light levels are measured by units called footcandles. For example, we know that a 50 year old is probably going to be most comfortable with the general lighting in the kitchen if the room's footcandles are measured at about 30 to 40 (Task lighting will need significantly higher footcandles, and art lighting needs about five times higher footcandles than ambient light).

To achieve the ideal footcandle level, let's first assume that I'm using compact fluorescent lamps (commonly referred to as bulbs in the consumer market place) in the recessed down lights, otherwise known as cans or pots.

Oh, quit your howling, and sit tight. I'll tell you why I think that's the most practical kitchen light in a minute.

I'd need to know the length, width, ceiling height of the room and work surface height (36" high counters are standard in kitchens, unless you're unusually short or tall and you adjusted the counter height for comfort). Using these dimensions, I'd use an equation that tells me the Room Cavity Ratio (RCR). Then, knowing the reflectance values of the ceiling, walls, and floor in percentages, and the actual fixtures I want to use, I'd check the manufacturer specifications to get the Coefficient of Utilization number (CU). This number indicates how much light actually reaches the work surface as a percentage of the total light produced by the fixture. Depending on the material of the inside of the pot light for example, some of the light that comes out of the lamp will be absorbed before it ever has a chance to hit the work surface.

So now that I know the RCR, the CU, and the desired footcandles, I need to look at the manufacturer's specifications on the actual lamps. All lamps are not created equal, and they each put out a different number of lumens, a much more precise measurement of light than watts. Watts measure energy consumed; lumens measure the volume of light produced. So finding the lamp that will fit the fixture that I want, with the highest number of lumens, will tell me how far apart the lights should be spaced to end up with even general lighting. The higher the lumens, the fewer the fixtures I'll need in the ceiling, which is good since I don't want my clients' ceilings to look like Swiss cheese.

Types of lighting

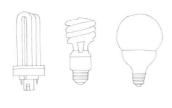

Compact fluorescent

If the words "fluorescent lighting" make you cringe, as you recall annoying lighted tubes buzzing and humming away in an overheated classroom until your being is pervaded by a persistent malaise and vague, unshakable nausea, listen up. Before you leap to conclusions about fluorescent lighting, let me turn those old perceptions on their antiquated heads.

Good fluorescent lamps come in various "color temperatures." Some appear warm, others cool. A compact fluorescent lamp (CFL) that you buy off the shelf at the lighting store, the kind with the screw base that you have been told should replace your energy-gobbling incandescent bulbs, will probably have the description "warm" or "cool" on the box to indicate whether its color spectrum is closer to the blue tones or the yellow tones. Most warm fluorescents tend toward pink rather than yellow, which is why many people don't like them. They have a cool hue.

The compact fluorescent bulbs that a lighting designer will specify and provide have a "dedicated base," enabling us to regulate the color temperature more precisely. The color temperature is measured numerically in degrees Kelvin (K) which tells us how warm or cool the light appears, and a numerical Color Rendering Index (CRI) which compares how accurately an artificial light source renders perceived colors as compared to daylight. The CFL bulb that is the closest match to standard incandescent has a color temperature of 2700 K and a CRI of 82.

A fluorescent lamp with a dedicated base usually has three or four pins on the bottom. In this case, the ballast, which is the device which regulates the flow of electricity into the bulb, is in the fixture, so you can have them on a dimmer. The fluorescent bulbs you get in the store have the familiar looking screw base with a bulbous neck. That knob on the neck is the ballast and can't be dimmed.

When you have compact fluorescent pot lights as your main source of kitchen light, you can use fewer fixtures and consume less energy and still get the same amount of light. For example, a 32w CFL puts out a comparable amount of light as a 150w incandescent, and it lasts an average of 10,000 hours (at five hours every single day that's about 5 and a half years). The average life of an incandescent is only about 1,000 hours. Over its lifetime, one CFL will save you about $75 in energy costs, plus you'll save the cost of 10 incandescent bulbs!

Unlike fluorescent pot lights, incandescent and halogen lighting both create bright spots or shadows on your work surface demanding that your eyes constantly re-adjust to the variable light. Track lighting is the worst if your track is mounted in the middle of the ceiling, as it lights the back of your head and creates shadows on the countertop. Still, I must admit, that a room solely lit by fluorescent pot lights, even with the right color temperature and CRI, can lack warmth. We can rectify this by layering the light. Adding decorative pendent fixtures with halogen bulbs over an island or peninsula will immediately "warm up" the color temperature and make it balanced. Another way to inject warmth into the room is with halogen or xenon (zee-non) lighting under the wall cabinets. Add to this some low voltage halogen directional lights in the ceiling to highlight a piece of wall art or display items and presto! You now have a space with warm light illuminating the room to optimal levels at all hours of the day.

Halogen

One myth about halogen bulbs is that they are all low-voltage. Not so. The halogen gas inside the bulb makes it burn whiter than incandescent, but not necessarily more efficiently. Some operate at 12 volts but some run on the same voltage as incandescent, 120 volts, also known as line voltage. Some halogen bulbs have a screw base, for example a par-20 or par-38 (these look like a bulb that you might put in an outdoor flood light) and some are the small bulbs that look like a low-voltage MR-16 (the small halogen bulbs with the two-pin base), but also use 120 volts. If you use these instead of the low voltage ones, typically the fixture that houses the bulbs is less expensive, since it doesn't require a built-in transformer to convert the electrical current from the standard 120 volts to the low 12 volts. The color of light is a little whiter, the wattage is a little lower but they are not particularly energy efficient.

The low-voltage lamps and fixtures do save energy using a lower voltage and a lower wattage, typically 50w as opposed to 75w or 100w. The standard low-voltage, MR-16 lamp available on the market has a life of between 2,500 and 4,000 hours. Ushio is the one manufacturer I know of whose MR-16s last an average of 10,000 hours.

Any MR-16 type lamp can be problematic, so it's not my first choice. The placement of the fixtures for MR-16 lamps must be calculated carefully. If they are too far apart, you'll get shadows on the countertop, if too close together, the light beams overlap, creating hot spots.

If you happen to buy a bulb with a narrower beam angle, the bulb will seem much brighter than the others. The characteristic of either low or line voltage is that the light itself is regulated by a beam which is emitted from the lamp. A wide beam distributes the light from the bulb over a wider area so that by the time the light hits the work surface, it is somewhat diffused. But you have to calculate the placement of the other fixtures carefully so they are not too far apart, otherwise there will be a perceptible shadow on the counter-top, which creates the hot and cool spots I was describing earlier. If, on the other hand they are placed too close together, the beam of light overlaps too much creating an even hotter spot than directly below the bulb, since light is cumulative. The optimal placement is achieved with a series of mathematical equations. Now, where the design gets really mucked up is when you have to replace one bulb and not the others, and by mistake you get a new bulb with a narrower beam angle, you will notice that this bulb seems much brighter than the ones around it, because its light is concentrated in a tighter area. Bulbs lose their intensity over time and a tighter beam angle means a more concentrated amount of light on the surface below it. To my eye, that creates a nasty, distracting variation of dark and light spots. The quality of light shouldn't leap out and literally hit you in the eye, but should just, well…be.

If you've ever made the mistake of looking up at a low voltage halogen light on the ceiling, you'll remember the UFO-type spots you saw swimming before your eyes. Thus, the second reason I prefer other types of lighting: the quality of low voltage halogen light is too intense and can be very unforgiving for general lighting. It highlights every imperfection on the walls or cabinet finish. Many people use the type of fixture that houses the bulb face flush with the ceiling. This creates a very strong glare that takes attention away from the aesthetics of the room and is a strain on aging eyes which don't adjust to changing light levels as quickly as younger eyes, so this struggle to adjust can cause headaches.

The third reason I personally hate low voltage lighting as general lighting in the kitchen, is that changing the bulbs is a major hassle. You don't just screw them out and in. You usually have to pull the trim out of the ceiling to access the receptacle into which you have to plug two itty bitty little pins into two miniscule teeny, tiny holes in the wee little fixture that's too small to get your fingers into, all while standing on a chair or ladder and craning your neck at an awkward angle until the connection is made. If you keep your kitchen lights turned on an average of five and a half hours a day, you're going to go through that rigamarole every 18 months, multiplied by the number of light fixtures you have. See how pure you can keep your language while doing that!

The 2 ½" PAR-20 bulbs with the screw base are easier to change than the bi-pins, but they only come with a narrow beam angle, requiring you to use more of them closer together to eliminate ghastly shadowing on the work surface. They are typically only 50w, so use less energy per fixture than the 60w or 75w incandescent with comparable light. But because you need more of them, the energy savings are negated. They also have a relatively short life.

LED

LED is an acronym for Light Emitting Diode. All light bulbs used for residential lighting that are not LED have a filament, or tiny thin coiled wire within the bulb, which heats up and glows, creating light. Over time, the heat burns through the filament, breaking the connection, causing the bulb to die. The LED has no filament to burn out, so its life is many thousands of hours longer than most other light sources, usually an average of up to 35,000 to 50,000 hours. The energy consumption is tiny compared to other bulbs, so

TALES FROM THE TRENCHES

Using my home and showroom as my laboratory to try new design ideas and products didn't stop with the cork floor. In my own kitchen is where I first tried CFL pot lights layered with incandescent pendent lights over the island, halogen under cabinet lights, and low voltage halogen directional lights highlighting a display cabinet and wall hung art. When I first installed the fluorescents in 2001, the contractor, electrician, and others all thought I was nuts. No one in my area had applied fluorescent pot lights for residential use. Low voltage halogen fixtures were all the rage, but then as now, I was convinced they were not the best solution for general lighting.

After some trial and error, fitting the proper sized bulb to the right fixture, I discovered what I believe to be an optimum lighting formula for kitchens, my light layering technique. In 99% of the homes that I've used this technique, the clients give it rave reviews.

Dark colored cabinets at eye level will absorb high levels of ambient light, so the room will need more lumens not to feel gloomy. This room is well lit, resulting in the dark cabinets having visual punch against the light backgrounds of the floor, counter & backsplash.

Merit Kitchens

the savings are huge. It also doesn't generate as much heat as other lamps, so it won't affect the heating or cooling cycle of the room.

LED technology is widely-used in fixtures like exit and emergency signs which are constantly lit so need a long life and low cost. They can be successfully used as recessed wall lights to light stairs or pathways, and their efficiency is not affected by the cold as is fluorescent technology.

All this sounds like the ideal light source except as far as I have seen, LED technology is simply not advanced enough yet to effectively light a room with ambient lighting unless you use approximately twice the number of fixtures to compensate for the lack of lumens.

To get an idea of the difference in light output of various kinds of bulbs, have a look at the following light chart (the lumens are approximate – actual lumen output for 50w bulbs may vary from manufacturer to manufacturer).[8]

NOTE: Watts are units of energy consumed and lumens are units of light emitted which is how you tell how bright the light is. The types of bulbs are listed below in ascending order of wattage. But note that the highest wattage bulb (the 100w incandescent) does not put out the highest number of lumens. That award goes to the 26w compact fluorescent.

[8] Retrieved from Light Calc lighting program by Enviro-Systems, Jan 11, 2009
www.lightcalc.com

This chart is a simplified comparison of bulb types. There are many more factors that go into determining the appropriate bulb for the job. Although lighting preferences are subjective, perhaps you can now see why I am a fan of the CFL bulb.

WATT	BULB TYPE	LUMENS	LIFE/HRS
3w	MR-16 LED (equivalent to 20w)	210	20,000
12w	PAR-38 LED (equivalent to a 50w MR-16)	960	20,000
26w	Compact fluorescent	1,800	10,000
50w	PAR-20 (needs a 4" aperture)	560	750
50w	MR-16 (bi-pin, low voltage halogen)	960	4,000
60w	PAR-38 (screw base. Needs a 7" aperture)	1150	2,000
75w	MR-16 (bi-pin, low voltage halogen)	1400	4,000
100w	A-19 (regular incandescent)	1715	1,000

No matter what type of light you prefer, energy conservation must be a primary consideration. Several jurisdictions in North America have passed laws requiring fluorescents to be the primary source of lighting in the kitchen, and the trend is spreading. As you see in the chart above, incandescent is inefficient. It's actually a better source of heat than light, as more than 80% of its energy is transmuted into heat! Since Thomas Edison patented the light bulb in 1879,[9] the plain old light bulb has been the main source of light for homes. Incandescent bulbs are familiar, easy to find, cheap to buy, and a no-brainer to install, so people are reluctant to give them up. But these days we must be conscious of how we use energy, even if it requires trying something new.

[9] "Contrary to popular belief, Edison didn't "invent" the light bulb, but rather he improved upon a 50-year-old idea. In 1879, using lower current electricity, a small carbonized filament, and an improved vacuum inside the globe, he was able to produce a reliable, long-lasting source of light. Edison's eventual achievement was inventing not just an incandescent electric light, but also an electric lighting system that contained all the elements necessary to make the incandescent light practical, safe, and economical. After one and a half years of work, success was achieved when an incandescent lamp with a filament of carbonized sewing thread burned for thirteen and a half hours. The first public demonstration of Edison's incandescent lighting system was in December 1879, when the Menlo Park laboratory complex was electrically lighted. Edison spent the next several years creating the electric industry. http://inventors.about.com/library/inventors/bledison.htm

Appliances

CHAPTER 7

APPLIANCES

For many people, sorting through a myriad of choices in manufacturers, features, and price points makes choosing appliances an agonizing, bewildering process.

The best time to start shopping for appliances is AFTER the designer has done a concept drawing for the new layout. This way, the designer can give you guidelines as to how much space you can spare for each appliance while still giving you enough working countertop and storage space. In a small kitchen, a 48" wide fridge and a 36" wide cook top with double wall ovens may eliminate all work areas and storage space. You must weigh in practicality and safety with your appliance preferences before you buy.

Resist all temptation to buy your appliances before your kitchen design has begun. Even if there's a fantastic sale going on, DON'T DO IT!! You could box yourself into a design corner and lose the flexibility to achieve the optimum layout.

Appliance color is another reason to wait until you have a sense of how the whole kitchen design is going to play out. You will find numerous articles in magazines and newspapers cautioning you against picking wild appliance colors, citing the hideous Harvest Gold, Avocado Green, and Unmentionable Brown of the 1970s. Pardon me for being blunt, but that's a ridiculous argument.

Those colors were highly fashionable in the 1970s (a whole decade that demonstrated monstrously bad taste), and by the time those colors fell out of favor, the appliances needed to be replaced anyway. More to the point, colored appliances should work with the overall kitchen concept, so they don't look like a gigantic spaceship landed in the room. It all comes back to what I talked about earlier in the color section: if you love it, incorporate it, and you will love it until the whole thing is ready to be replaced. Nothing stays in style forever, and that includes appliances. The white fridge of 1950 looks completely different from the white fridge of today. The color is only part of the issue.

Cooking equipment and ventilation

Jenn-Air

Specialty finishes on appliances like this bronze finish can become the dominant color element in the room

There is no other appliance that inspires such strong opinions or arguments as cooking equipment, whether that is the cook top, oven, grill, or steam oven.

For my purposes here, a cook top is an appliance with burners, either gas, electric, or induction, which is not attached to an oven. It might be stealthy, sleek, and unobtrusive with a glass top and electronic controls that sits flush with the countertop, or it might be what I call the MACK truck of cook tops, which has the controls on the front of a chunky stainless steel panel. It breaks the line of the countertop edge to protrude beyond it and commands attention with its presence, muscle, and heft. Neither is better or worse than the other in terms of style; it depends on the style of the kitchen and what look you wish to achieve.

Many serious cooks swear by gas burners stating that they are hottest, easiest to regulate by sight, and instantly turn on and off. But not all gas cook tops are created equal. Some burn hotter than others (measured in BTU's or British Thermal Units, just like a gas furnace) and some have continuous burner grates, which serves up an easy way of sliding cooking vessels between burners rather than lifting. Some gas cook tops have sealed burners (keeping spills away from the guts of the unit), and some don't.

Although traditionally gas has been the fuel of choice for serious cooks, induction is gaining momentum. With induction, the **cooking vessel itself generates the cooking heat.**[10] When an induction burner comes into contact with a magnetic vessel such as cast iron or steel (NOT stainless), the electromagnetic energy generated by the induction

[10] Retrieved from www.theinductionsite.com
January 11/09

burner makes the vessel hot, but keeps the burner only warm to the touch. The heat comes from the vessel transferring it to the burner, not the other way around.

The disadvantage to this kind of cook top is that your stainless steel, aluminum, copper, or Pyrex® pots and pans won't work. Cooking vessels must be ferrous (containing iron) metal to conduct the magnetic energy. But the huge advantage is that water boils faster on an induction range than any other kind of cook top, and as soon as you turn the burner off, the heat is instantly off, although the vessel will stay hot for a period of time, as it would using a traditional heat source. The interesting thing about induction is that it delivers about 85-90% of its energy to the cooking process, while gas loses at least half its energy to the atmosphere. So looking at it strictly as a physics experiment (don't worry, this is as close to a physics lecture as I'm gonna get), induction is the most energy efficient means of cooking.

Good old electric cook tops come in a few varieties including the familiar coil burner, the lowest priced option, and the halogen, which heats up a glass top burner much faster than a traditional coil, is easier to clean, and cools down more quickly. The glass top cook tops and ranges are easier to maintain than when they were first introduced. Because the surface is smooth without many crevices, they clean up easily with a quick wipe. For baked on food, many come with a special scraper that won't mar the surface. They have the aesthetic advantage of an unobtrusive look, which may be desirable if your kitchen is in view of the living or dining area of your home.

The same hood in two different finishes can set the tone for the style of the room

This hood uses a cabinet above to hide the duct.

Ventilation

All cook tops and ranges should be well ventilated, preferably to the outdoors. Before today's strict building codes, budget-priced homes were outfitted with a fan in the ceiling roughly in the vicinity of the stove. This was only slightly more effective than if you'd put a hole in your living room ceiling to extract smoke from your fireplace. More sophisticated appliances have increased the need for proper ventilation. Cooking with high heat and combustible energy requires that fumes and smoke be extracted efficiently and moisture buildup eliminated. The efficacy of a vent hood is measured in the amount of air extracted in cubic feet per minute (CFM). A high powered extractor fan (1,100 CFM) is most appropriate for a professional gas range, whereas a low powered fan (around 250 CFM) doesn't get rid of moisture build up from steam, and is useful only for a small electric range where heavy duty cooking is not the norm.

Most often, the vent is located over the cook top, since cooking grease, smoke, and fumes rise and are most easily captured above the source. However, if it isn't practical or would be especially unsightly to have a vent above the cook top, another option is a down draft. On a four burner unit, the down draft is sometimes placed in the centre of the unit, or can sit at the back and rise when it's on and retract out of sight when it's off. A down draft needs to have a high CFM to be effective, and it's not the best option with gas because too much heat is sucked down the vent.

I happen to like the appliances in view. I don't feel the need to camouflage the vent with cabinetry or specially designed housings. To me, an exposed vent says, "A good cook uses this kitchen." However, since most exposed vents are made of stainless steel, some with a combination of glass, they may not be the best aesthetic choice in a traditionally styled kitchen. In that case, the cabinet maker or manufacturer can usually provide matching or contrasting cabinetry components to hide the hood.

One camouflage option I can't stand is the "mantle hood." Made of manufactured stone or wood products to match the cabinetry, it has "legs" that come down to the countertop on either side of the cook top. It looks like a miniature fireplace mantel, hence its name. Unless you have a clear run of at least 10' of counter top with the cook top in the middle, the legs of the mantel will obstruct your counter landing space and prevent you from laying out plates and ingredients directly next to the cook top. This style is very popular with people who want their kitchen to look "posh," but it's ridiculously impractical. There are better, more user-friendly ways to create a ritzy look. I loathe a show-off kitchen that doesn't work.

Wood-Mode

A mantel hood can make a dramatic focal point but be sure there is enough counter space on either side of the range for efficiency.

Ovens

Ovens are the "boxes" you bake and roast in. They are not "stoves." Stove is the antiquated term for a self-supporting, free-standing unit that housed both the cook top and the oven. Those types of units still exist of course, but most are far more sophisticated than their predecessors (unless you're buying the bargain basement model). Today, the popular term is "range."

The oven, whether in a range or in a deep eye-level cabinet can be either electric or gas. Ovens can be radiant, convection, or a combination of the two. Radiant heat is as the name suggests, a coil either on top or the bottom of the oven cavity (or both), which heats up to red hot and radiates the heat to the whole oven. Convection ovens use a combination of radiant heat and a fan to move the heat around the oven, which often speeds cooking time.

These days, most people insist on a self-cleaning oven, but I'm not sold on the concept. To self-clean, the oven temperature must go up over 500 degrees for an extended period of time, essentially reducing the splattered grease and food on the walls of the oven to ash, which can be wiped up afterward. However, the exorbitant amount of energy consumed for this action makes the practice questionable, and the unit is inoperable during the cleaning period which can take several hours. On the other hand, spray-on oven cleaners use caustic chemicals to dissolve baked-on grease. What effects do those chemicals have on your indoor air quality and the environment when the sponge is rinsed and cleaning supplies are discarded? It's a tricky situation with no optimal solution. You'll have to let your own conscience guide you.

In large modern kitchens you'll often see a tall, deep cabinet with two ovens stacked on top of one another, with a warming drawer at the bottom of the stack. This gives maximum flexibility, so you can simultaneously bake, roast, and keep something warm. While this is enormously appealing to many people, some kitchens simply aren't big enough to accommodate this kind of arrangement without sacrificing much needed counter space.

Dacor

Install the oven, microwave drawer, and warming drawer in a single tall cabinet to save space.

In smaller kitchens where space is tight, I frequently suggest that clients add a convection microwave in addition to a single oven. Some microwave manufacturers make models that can switch to a convection bake mode and can be used as a conventional oven when not being used as a microwave, so you get two separate appliances in the space of one. The downside, of course, is that their functions cannot be used concurrently as separate units can, but it's still a pretty good compromise.

The steam oven, an interesting innovation in recent years, is the size of a microwave and gets built into a deep cabinet. It cooks food with steam instead of radiant or convection heat, so you don't need to add fat or oil. Wonderful for cooking fish and many vegetables but it's not so great for a steak. Still, if you have the room and the budget, it's a nice thing to have.

Miele

The height of the homeowners can determine the optimum height of appliances like this steam oven and gas cooktop.

One innovation I hope to see in the near future is a microwave oven with a choice of hinge sides. Conventional microwaves typically only hinge on the left when you're facing them. Why is it a fridge can have a door hinge on the side that best suits its orientation in the room, but not a microwave? Some microwaves have doors that hinge at the bottom like an oven door, but they have to be installed low enough, so the door isn't an obstruction or a danger to kids or short people like me (5'-2").

Microwave drawers are, in my opinion, the most interesting advancement in microwaves. They are installed beneath the countertop and open like a drawer, so that you view the contents from above, instead of at eye level. This is a fantastic help in many kitchens where wall space is so tight we can't afford to sacrifice wall cabinet storage space to install a microwave.

Dacor

A microwave drawer allows you to functionally install the microwave under the counter saving wall and cabinet space

Another choice is called a speed oven. It's a cross between a regular oven and a microwave. One European manufacturer has a product that uses a combination of microwaves and radiant heat to cook the food at a much faster rate than a conventional oven, yet it still has browning capabilities. Since microwaves are part of the cooking process, metal pans cannot be used. The North American brand uses infrared heat which is faster than radiant heat, can use metal pans, and is less expensive than its European counterpart. Take note of the voltage required for the receptacle. Some require 220 volts rather than the standard 120 volts.

No matter which kind of microwave you use, one thing is for darn sure: there is no excuse for a new kitchen in which the microwave sits on the counter. Anyone doing your kitchen who doesn't find a way to build in your microwave should be voted off the island!

Refrigeration

If there's anything that gives me the chills, it's a 28" deep, 30" wide side-by-side fridge (freezer on the left and fridge on the right). Don't talk to me about cubic footage. In terms of everyday use and practicality, cubic footage doesn't say squat. A side-by-side fridge of the dimensions I

Elmira Stove Works

Retro styling and vivid color can bring as much style as function to the room.

Sub Zero

A glass door on the fridge is a strong reference to restaurant style, but you may not want all your leftovers on view.

gave above won't be wide enough to store any kind of platter on the fridge side, and will be so deep, your leftovers will sprout legs and attack before you can make your way to the back to see what's lurking there. The freezer is not bad in a fridge like this, and it surely beats the old-fashioned kind with the piddly box freezer on the top.

My recommendation to clients is a side-by-side fridge should be at least 48" wide. A built in fridge is more shallow, and needs the extra width to give a family of four enough refrigerator space. And even then, you may want to keep a separate unit for space gobblers such as soft drinks, juices, and snacks.

TALES FROM THE TRENCHES

Although I blush to admit it, when I re-designed the kitchen for our house, I specified a food waste disposer for the sink. At that time, we did not have a municipal composting program which has since been put into place. I disliked the idea of wet food waste sitting in the trash can along with non-recyclable packaging, and I reasoned that pulverizing it and sending it down the drain would start it on its way to a water treatment plant before it was sent out into the lake. I didn't realize then that in my city, only waste water from toilets gets directed to the water treatment plants, and that what goes down the sink drain goes straight into the lake. In a city of 4 million people, even if only 2 million send food straight into the lake, that is too much of a load. The impact is noticeable. When it rains and the water is choppy, the pollution gets stirred up, and no one can swim in the lake.

One day, I was preparing dinner for 15 people and turned on the garburator, only to be horrified as disgusting, black mucky water started backing up in my sink and continued to rise covering the whole counter top and overflowing onto the floor! The emergency plumber explained that starchy and sticky waste like potato and carrot peelings get stuck to the side of the canister and accumulate rather than getting ground up and going down the drain. A disposer with a reverse action can minimize this. However, since then, I have been a dedicated composter.

If you really think about how often you use your fridge versus your freezer, a refrigerator with the freezer on the bottom provides a distinct advantage. During the course of preparing a meal, you might open and close the fridge door three times as often as the freezer; therefore it makes great sense to have the fridge at eye level and the freezer below, as secondary cooling. A freezer with an automatic ice maker is a terrific convenience. If you're like me, and never remember to fill up the ice trays, this will ensure that every time you reach into the freezer, you will come out with a fist full of ice.

A counter depth, built-in fridge is a great space saver in a small kitchen. A fridge that protrudes into the room visually dominates: not an attractive sight. When the fridge has cabinetry panels on the front, referred to as décor panels, the fridge is even less obtrusive; but not all fridges can accommodate these panels. Be sure to check before you buy. A counter depth fridge often makes up in organization what it lacks in depth, and personally, I'll never go back to a deep fridge again.

One new development, refrigerated drawers, can be located on an island away from the main preparation area and used to hold drinks and snacks for easy access. It can also be located in a pantry or a bar area to hold drink mix. When used in concert with a bar sink and wine cooler, it makes for a very flexible and practical bar area.

Another new feature gaining popularity is the French door fridge, with two side-by-side doors on top opening to the fridge compartment, with a freezer below. This allows a fridge installation in a space without enough room for a full depth door swing.

Dacor

A French door fridge cuts the space needed for a door swing in half which can be a big benefit in a tight kitchen.

Since many people prefer to entertain in the kitchen these days, placing a wine cooler in the kitchen can be a practical solution if you have a large enough area. Just be sure it's placed away from the prep and cooking zone, so there are no collisions. A cooler with a glass panel door should have ultraviolet protection to prevent the wine from spoiling in the sunlight. A good wine cooler has separate temperature zones for red and white wine and low vibration, as vibration can upset the balance of a fine wine. If you aren't a serious oenophile, there are also basic models on the market which may be perfectly adequate for your needs.

Trash compactors/food waste disposers

I admit a personal bias, but I have a philosophical problem with both these appliances. But let me describe them, then we'll talk about whether you really want one or not.

A trash compactor is a pull out drawer with an electronic mechanism that does exactly as its name suggests: compacts trash. If you have a large family, this may be a practical gadget for refuse that can't be recycled or composted. You can stuff several times as much garbage into a smaller package. And that's my problem with it. I'm just not crazy about the thought of the same garbage stinking up my kitchen for many days without being taken out. More important is the environmental concern. If we all responsibly recycle and compost to cut down on the amount of waste going into the landfill, a compactor is unnecessary. But the reality is that not every area has recycling or composting programs in place and until we demand that manufacturers dramatically cut down on packaging, there will still be excess trash to toss. Still, if you live in an apartment or a townhome with no protected outdoor area to store your garbage it may work for you.

A pinnacle vent that rises up from under the counter behind the cooktop can eliminate the need for an overhead hood.

Another environmentally questionable way to dispose of kitchen waste is the food waste disposer, or garburator as it's known in my area. The food goes down the sink drain into a grinder in the cabinet beneath and pulverizes food waste, so it can be washed down the drain. The problem with this is that in most municipalities, this sink waste goes into the storm sewers and into a nearby body of water, or if you're on a septic system, it goes into your tank. Either way, it can over-tax the system and cause environmental issues.

Small countertop appliances

Modern kitchens often have a plethora of small appliances that create storage problems. Things like a coffee maker, food processor, blender, toaster, toaster oven, bread maker, pasta maker, stand mixer, rice cooker, countertop griddle, or waffle iron. Most of these items don't come in built-in models (except the coffee makers), so be sure you tell your designer which of these things you use daily, so they can be placed for easy access without cluttering up the counter.

If you're shy about using built-in appliances in colors other than basic white, black, or stainless steel, here's your chance to have some fun. Highlight some of the colors you're using in the room with countertop appliances. If you really get tired of the color, you can always move it to a cabinet.

A 48" high glass door display cabinet hides the cooktop and pinnacle vent when fully extended.

A fridge like this Sub Zero 700 series full refrigerator with drawers, allows it to be completely clad with panels. To achieve an authentic vintage ice-box look, reproduction handles were custom forged and panels were designed to look like ice box doors.

How Green
Is Your Kitchen

CHAPTER 8

HOW GREEN IS YOUR KITCHEN?

Food for thought:

A man in the vegetable section of the grocery store asked the clerk if the organic vegetables had been sprayed with poisonous chemicals. The clerk replied, "No sir. You'll have to do that yourself."

Eco-friendly, "green" design is one of the most important developments to hit the kitchen business since we expunged avocado green appliances. If you have not yet jumped on the green bandwagon, then you're still in the dark ages where green refers only to vegetables. The U.S. and Canadian Green Building Councils have established a LEED (Leadership in Energy and Environmental Design) program for homes, but it is meant for new construction and doesn't yet apply to renovation, so I won't get into it here.

"Green" is everywhere. Open any design or décor magazine; read the newspaper homes sections; go to any bookstore with a well stocked design section; the titles and articles on environmentally friendly design abound. Google lists about 180 million matches when you search "green design." Everyone wants to proclaim their greenery to "leaf" the competition in the dirt. Products proclaim to be greener than envy. But are their claims bio-debatable?

Air pollution comes in from the cold

The EPA and Health Canada have found that indoor air can be *significantly* more polluted than air outdoors[11] and most of us spend 90% of our time indoors. The indoor air quality can be affected by mold, mildew, and VOCs (volatile organic compounds) from various materials and finishes. You don't have to have the nose of a bloodhound to smell the strong, often noxious odor when a new kitchen cabinet order is unwrapped, or a room has been freshly painted, or a granite countertop has been freshly sealed.

Product off gassing adversely affects indoor air quality to the extent that 40% of all children currently suffer from disorders like asthma, allergies, and other illness, all likely caused by poor indoor air quality and constant exposure to toxic chemicals in house cleaning and personal care products, as well as surface finishes. Materials don't have to be cheap to be hazardous. An affluent consumer who lavishly spends money on all the coolest materials and finishes could have dangerous indoor air conditions. Recurring headaches, a persistent cough, sleep disorders, and general lack of well-being are possibly attributable to poor air quality in our homes.

The kitchen business has been slow to join the green movement. Manufacturers are driven by consumer demand, and consumers have not yet spoken loudly enough to prompt widespread change. Mind you, most manufacturers want you to *think* they've gone green and make lots of self-congratulating claims to try to capture market share. Some companies have taken steps to improve their green status by using wood approved by The Forest Stewardship Council (FSC). The FSC is "an independent,

non-governmental, not for profit organization established to promote the responsible management of the world's forests."*12* VOC incineration with sophisticated filter systems eliminate the majority of the toxins before they reach the atmosphere outside the manufacturing facility. But these methods and processes are expensive, generating costs which must be passed on to the consumer. Although many consumers love the *idea* of going green, if it's more expensive, by and large, they still prefer to keep the green in their wallets.

Where's the proof?

Regardless of out of pocket cost, we are all going to have to get serious about buying sustainable and responsible products. The scientific evidence shows that we are literally abusing our planet to death. Al Gore's film, *An Inconvenient Truth*, sounded a wake up call, yet naysayers persist in denying the evidence. It reminds me of the mid-twentieth century, when tobacco companies swore that cigarette smoking was harmless. I think we can all now safely say that smoking cigarettes poses certain health risks. And I'm sure that the science in Gore's film has some holes in it, but even if a fraction of the information presented in the film is accurate, every single one of us has to change our behavior. Sooner or later, we all are going to have to wake up and smell the greenery and make some very hard choices about the way we live, manufacture, and consume, or be forced into change by an eco-system collapse. And if we allow it to collapse, it will be too late for the naysayers to say "Oops, my bad," and it will be way too late for "I told you so."

12The Forest Stewardship Coucil website (2008)
www.fsc.org

The green product pool

In my mind, there's no question we need to be concerned about the environment and support manufacturers who produce green products. The issue is, are we truly getting green products, or is it all just "green washing," a marketing bonanza to trumpet green products, deliberately misleading the consumer to believe that a product or process is more environmentally responsible than it is? It's not always easy to tell, so we each must educate ourselves and read between the lines, read the labels, and ask the right questions. For example, while some materials may be inherently green, the finishing process may not be. There may be compounds added to increase performance or durability that are not entirely green, so you have to weigh the pros and cons of your purchase.

Globalization of the world's economies is actually a contributing factor to environmental problems. Although it's appealing to be able to say that one's kitchen cabinets are from Germany, the slate on the floor is from Brazil, and the marble of the countertop is from Italy, buying local is the way of the future. Transporting products from far-flung locations consumes huge quantities of fuel. The packaging to protect those products are often non-recyclable and end up in landfills. Still, sometimes it's worth it, if the difference in quality is significant.

The effort required to change our collective mindset toward environmental preservation is a little like turning a 500 foot barge around 180 degrees. It doesn't happen quickly. It takes time. The important thing is to start, while implementing as many changes as possible during the transition. When given a choice, pick the more responsible material whenever you can.

Above all, don't think that your small contribution won't make a difference so you needn't bother. And, remember, there comes a point when ignorance ends and negligence begins.

Here are some guidelines:

When demolishing the kitchen, specify that all materials, whenever possible, should be recycled, reused, or donated. Some organizations will take your reusable kitchen

Food for thought:

"Never doubt that a small group of thoughtful, committed citizens can change the world. Indeed, it is the only thing that ever has."
- Margaret Mead

cabinets, countertops, plumbing fixtures, and other materials, resell them and give you a tax receipt. Do an internet search to find a program in your area. One of my personal favorites is Habitat for Humanity.

Cut down on VOCs. Choose a cabinetry manufacturer that the Kitchen Cabinet Manufacturers Association (KCMA) has certified as meeting its "Environmental Stewardship Program" (ESP) standards. In 2006, the KCMA created the program to help cabinet manufacturers demonstrate their commitment to environmental sustainability and enable consumers to easily identify environmentally-friendly products. After meeting certification requirements in areas of air quality, product and process resource management, environmental stewardship, and community relations, cabinet manufacturers may display the ESP seal on their products, helping you identify which cabinet manufacturers are committed to protecting the environment. Nearly 120 cabinet manufacturers have earned ESP certification, and more are completing the review process.[13]

Some cabinet manufacturers use formaldehyde-free particle board or plywood for the cabinet core and some are opting for wheat board or straw board instead, some of which use soy-based glues. Ask what type of finish is on the exposed surfaces. Sometimes there's a trade-off between an environmentally friendly finish and durability. For the backsplash, look for recycled glass tile that you can mount with a non-toxic glue. Terazzo countertops use a combination of recycled glass and concrete base. Try to use paint with low VOCs. You can buy paint that uses natural raw materials from responsibly managed sources with no petrochemicals or formaldehyde. Many established brands have a line of eco-friendly paints that are less toxic both for indoor air quality and when disposing of leftover product and cans. Some areas are even working to outlaw oil-based paints altogether.

Properly ventilate the kitchen. Use your hood fan every time you cook. Moisture buildup from cooking accumulates on surfaces and in crevices and can lead to a mold and mildew problem that your nose can't detect, but can be hazardous to your health.

Conserve water. Use water flow regulators on your faucet and Energy Star appliances. Don't let your water run to get a cold drink. Plan ahead and keep a pitcher full of cold drinking water in the fridge. Rather than let water go down the drain when waiting for it to get hot, collect it in a large pot or container and use it for cooking or to rinse hand-washed dishes or water indoor plants or the garden. Consider replacing the old dinosaur

[13] www.Greencabinetsource.org
retrieved October 21, 2009

in the basement that heats your water with a tankless water heater in the kitchen. Delivering hot water on-demand, it eliminates the need to maintain a constant 40-50 gallon supply of pre-heated water, and cuts down on water waste. You may be able to recycle used water by installing a grey water system, but first be aware of local regulations about how grey water may be collected and used. Barrels connected to eaves troughs can be an effective way to collect rain water to irrigate the garden.

Food for thought:

Water is arguably our most valuable resource. Is a low-quality $30 faucet which has no flow control or filtration the right way to manage our most valuable resource?

Use eco-friendly flooring materials. Bamboo and cork are natural, rapidly renewable resources. Linoleum is made up of linseed oil, lime, wood or cork flour, rosin and jute or canvas, so it's both recyclable and biodegradable. (Beware of a material which may be called linoleum, but is made of polyvinyl chloride (PVC), which can be highly toxic if burned.) Rubber tiles made of recycled tires are durable, easy to maintain, but not likely to be biodegradable. If you must install a wood floor, use FSC approved wood with a water-based finish, or better yet, tung or linseed oil finish. Or consider reclaimed wood from barns or river bottoms. They have character and a unique weathered beauty, and no new trees need be harvested. There is an interesting type of wood flooring made from re-cycling pallets used in shipping. In the past, these pallets were used one time and discarded, a terrible waste of wood and landfill space.

Recycled cotton made from blue jeans can be used instead of foam or fibreglass to insulate the exterior walls, but the vapor barrier must be perfect. If cotton insulation gets wet, it sucks up moisture and gets moldy very quickly.

Install fluorescent pot lights (properly specified, as described in the lighting chapter) as the main light source. It will save a significant amount of energy and provide efficient, shadow-free light. Look for low-mercury content bulbs. Put closet and walk-in pantry lights on automatic switches. Use dimmers on lights whenever possible. Dimming lights when full light isn't needed significantly prolongs the life of the bulb. Use LED lighting for under cabinet lights. It uses a fraction of the energy of every other type of lighting, does not generate heat, and has an incredibly long life; however, since it's fairly new technology, it's still expensive. Using light paint colors reflects more light therefore reduces the amount of energy needed to light the room.

Bamboo is a fast growing material, is durable,
attractive, and growing in popularity for kitchen floors.

Divert as much kitchen trash as you can away from landfills. In addition to the requisite built-in trash can, plan to install built-in recycling and compost bins. Take reusable bags to the grocery store, so you don't accumulate mountains of plastic bags that often end up in the trash. When you buy bags for your trash and compost bins, try to buy biodegradable.

I am a recent convert to the "movement." I have to confess I was once a green philistine. I am ashamed to admit that I sneered at the "tree huggers" wearing Birkenstocks and socks.

Many years ago, I was hired by a man who was building a gracious 10,000 square foot home on a horse farm in the country. He was prepared to spare no expense on cabinets, countertops, flooring, and backsplash to minimize toxic off-gassing. At that time, the green movement in interior design was still a pea in its pod, so the client knew more than I did. Though I was happy to oblige, I secretly wondered whether he might not be just a wee bit hysterical about this whole environmental thing. Now, I look back with admiration at the forward-thinking that led my client to push the boundaries of design and specification. I didn't realize until much later how much that experience raised my own consciousness.

I have become more aware of green materials and conserving energy. I do what I can to persuade my clients to choose environmentally responsible methods and materials. I brandish fluorescent prose from my strawboard soap box at every opportunity. Until LED technology is ready for general residential lighting, which at the time of this writing, it isn't, fluorescent is the best option for lighting the kitchen (I'm not advocating it for dining rooms or bedrooms, but both those areas use less energy to start with). And as for sending stuff to landfills, it sends me into orbit to hear about a kitchen in good condition that was ripped out and sent to our desperately over-burdened landfills when a home owner decided to remodel.

I am a ruthless crusader against bottled water – both the portable sizes and the giant bottles that get delivered to your door and plopped in a cooling unit. Bottled water for mass consumption is a crazy business. The suppliers capitalize on people's fears about the quality of municipal water. We have recently been made aware of the toxic chemicals from plastic containers that leach into the water that we are literally pouring into our bodies with a potentially disastrous effect. The companies that take water from underground springs and bottle it are removing millions of gallons a day from the earth, affecting resources that farmers often depend upon, using tons of fuel to run the factories and truck the bottles to locations remote from the source. And don't even get me started on the companies that use our tap water, put it through a filtration system and sell it back to us. I find it appalling.

According to the International Council of Bottled Water Associations, in 2003 153,083,000,000 liters of bottled water were produced worldwide, with an estimated value of $45,772,000,000. And that was then...we could easily be spending five times that in 2011. If you're worried about money right now, keep a diary of what you spend on bottled water per week and see how much you'd save if you turned on the tap instead. I bet you'll be shocked at the result. And what happens to those millions and billions of plastic bottles once we're done with them? Into the landfill. We throw them away without a thought...a very small percentage are recycled.

Buy a couple of stainless steel water bottles, fill them from the tap and keep them in the fridge to grab when you're on the go. It will save your wallet, your health and the earth.

Duro Design

Cork flooring is soft underfoot, comes in a variety of colours and natural patterns, and is a renewable resource. It's an environmentally friendly choice for your kitchen.

Getting Quotes
& Questions You
Should Ask

CHAPTER 9

GETTING QUOTES AND QUESTIONS YOU SHOULD ASK

O K. Finally, we're going to talk about the question you really wanted answered right away, but I made you wade through all the rest of the stuff first (kind of like your mother making you eat your vegetables before you dig into dessert): getting quotes to find out how much this whole thing is going to cost.

You've had the kitchen designed, you've got all the drawings, you've picked your materials and finishes and have the written scope of work, which specifies the work to be done item by item, and all of the products and model numbers written down and ready to go. Armed with this information you can get quotes. If all of the stuff I just mentioned was pulled together by an independent designer, you can shop it to various kitchen companies to get quotes for the cabinetry and countertops. Some will also be able to sell you plumbing fixtures, faucets, and other materials. Some will take on the construction, and some won't. But even if you need a separate quote from the contractor, at least everyone is working off the same documents, so you should have quotes that you can easily compare. You'll be comparing apples to apples, not apples to bananas.

If you used an independent company to design your kitchen, ask if they also do cabinetry and manage the renovation. If so, they can be one of the companies on your list. If not, ask if they can refer you to companies who do. The next best way to find kitchen companies to interview about your project is to talk to friends and relatives who have had a remodel done similar in size and scope to yours and get recommendations.

Visit the company's Web site first, then if you like what you see, to save time, give them a call before you go to their showroom. Have a list of questions to ask to decide if you want to go to the next step of going in to see them.

Here are some things you should ask (obviously, tailor the questions to your specific situation):

- I have a kitchen design and drawings that were done by an independent designer. Are you willing to work from these drawings?
- My budget is "x" for cabinets, countertop, sink, faucet, lighting, flooring, backsplash, and labor. Does this sound like a budget you could work with? And will that budget allow me to do any customizing of the cabinetry?
- Do you manage the whole process including the construction?
- Can I buy everything I'll need for the remodel through your company including appliances, flooring, countertop materials, sink, faucet, and lighting?
- Since we have detailed drawings and specifications done, how soon could we order cabinetry and what is your lead time?
- If you manage the construction process as well, how soon could you start a kitchen renovation where we are not moving any walls but are replacing everything else including lighting?
- Can you give me the names and phone numbers of 10 previous kitchen remodeling clients (anyone can give you three; it's harder to name 10 happy customers).
- Do you have any CKDs (Certified Kitchen Designers) on staff that I can deal with?

Investigate three or four different companies to ensure that you're getting a good cross section. Any more than that, and you may just get hopelessly confused. Once you've found three or four whose answers meet your criteria, make an appointment to go in and see them. This is important. If they tell you that you don't need an appointment, I'd be skeptical. A company that is organized and professional will want to know who is coming in and when, so they can be prepared. A busy company may not be able to give you the attention you deserve if you drop in unannounced. If you just want to have a look around, by all means drop in, but don't expect there to be someone there who is qualified to help you. It's a business, so make an appointment.

Be prepared for your appointment by bringing the drawings, a written list of work you want done, and any photos you've clipped out of magazines, to give the salesperson an idea of what you're looking for, then sit down and review the drawings and scope. Near the beginning of the appointment, talk about your budget to make sure the company will be able to accommodate you. They won't be able to commit to the exact price at that point, but they will certainly be able to tell you whether or not they can do a project like yours for that budget. If they say they can commit to the price right then, be very careful. They are just trying to grab a customer and lock them in. They don't yet have enough information to commit to a price. They should want to show you some of their cabinetry products to demonstrate the quality they offer, and show you some door styles and types of wood and finishes that they carry. Try to get them to show you a sample of something similar to what was specified in your drawings and scope of work and use that as the model to price from. Don't be tempted by a nicer door style, prettier color, or completely different wood. That will throw your price comparison all out of whack. You can make changes to those things after you've chosen a company.

If they can work within your budget, they should ask you to leave a copy of the drawings and scope with them. **<u>Make it clear that they are not to change anything.</u>** This is important so that when you are comparing quotes, you are comparing exactly the same thing. If something needs to be changed to accommodate the way they do things, or the products they sell, you can negotiate that item after you've hired them.

Price is not the only factor to consider when making your final choice. You will want to feel confident. If you feel uncomfortable in any way, listen to your gut, thank them for their time, and move on. The remodel process is long, dirty, messy, and full of frustration, and it will be much easier if you like the person who is managing the process.

Brent Foster

Panelling a wall with wood veneer can visually warm up an otherwise chilly space. Just remember that the material itself and labor to install it will add extra cost to the budget.

Living Through The Chaos, Be Prepared!

Food for thought:

CHAPTER 10

LIVING THROUGH THE CHAOS, BE PREPARED!

> "Home is an ever-evolving quest"
> - Ellen Cheever

Depending on the scope of your remodel, you could be without a functioning kitchen for months. If it's an extensive renovation with an addition or you're opening up the space to the rest of the house and your budget allows, it would be less stressful for the whole family if you move out of the house for at least the messiest part of the renovation.

But if you can't move out, you can only eat at friends' and relatives' so many times before you wear out your welcome, and eating out will devour your food budget fast. The best way to cope is to set up a makeshift kitchen somewhere else in the house where you can prepare basic meals and wash the dishes. Usually the most practical option is the laundry area (provided it's apart from your kitchen). A basement is sometimes a practical option away from the remodeling mess and near a water source.

In my business, I keep handy a spare 6' length of laminate countertop with a basic stainless steel sink and faucet installed in it that can be set up on saw horses and temporarily connected to the laundry sink. I also keep an extra microwave, toaster oven, electric kettle, hot plate, and electric frying pan to lend to my clients who don't already have these things, so they can function while camping out in the basement. Ask your kitchen company if they offer this service.

I'm going to assume that you're setting up a temporary kitchen in the basement. Move only the essentials down there and pack up the rest in labeled boxes and stash them in an empty corner. If you try to have every single thing from your kitchen available in your temporary space, the chaos will drive you crazy.

Here's a list of things you might want in your makeshift kitchen:

- **Dishes.** Don't bring the whole set down. You won't be having tea parties, so unless you use them on a daily basis, pack away tea cups and saucers and leave out a few mugs instead. The fewer dishes you have to wash, the better.

- **Cutlery.** Again, you may not need access to the whole set, but if they're in a plastic organizer tray, bring that down. The more cutlery you have available, the more tempting it is to reach for a clean one rather than keep washing just a few.

- **Carving knives and cooking utensils.** Just keep out a few sharp knives, basic cooking utensils, and a cutting board or two. Of course bring a few pots and pans to use on the hot plate, especially if you don't have an electric frying pan. A slow cooker can be a lifesaver during a renovation, since you can make a whole meal in one vessel and, depending on the size of your family, have enough to get you through a couple of days. It's unlikely you'll be baking a cake or making fancy dishes in your toaster oven and electric frying pan, so pack away your whisks, food processors, stand mixers, and other elaborate gadgetry.

- **Canned and dry goods.** To keep your meals simple and basic, canned and dry goods will really come in handy and can help minimize prep time. Don't forget the can opener!

- **Storage containers.** Keep a few available for leftovers. Or if you're really lucky and someone brings over a pot of soup or other yummy dish, decant it into your own container and give them their pot back!

- **Mixing and measuring.** You may want to do some basic mixing, like for scrambled eggs, so keep a couple of mixing bowls handy. A measuring cup would be a good idea too.

- **Dishwashing liquid.** You may be able to have your dishwasher temporarily hooked up downstairs. More than likely though, you'll have to wash dishes in the laundry sink. Have at hand a supply of detergent, rubber gloves, dish and hand towels and scrubby things.

- **Paper napkins.** There's no reason that manners have to go out the window just because you have to eat in the basement for a while.

If you already have a beverage fridge in the basement, move the beer to one side and use the rest for food storage for the duration of the remodel. If not, have your kitchen fridge moved to your interim kitchen. It may seem like a pain in the neck, but believe me, if you imagine having to run up and down the stairs to a fridge every time you need to get something out or put something back, you will appreciate the wisdom of this suggestion. If you can bring down your kitchen table and chairs and maybe a standing lamp to lighten the gloom, you won't be reveling in luxury, but you'll be able to survive the time out of your kitchen with a little less stress.

Clean out the garage!

You may think that taking everything out of the kitchen and surrounding rooms and piling them in the garage is a good way to get them out of the way, and I am now going to say a loud, firm NO!

During a remodel the garage is usually command central. It's often the only area where the contractor and carpenter can set up their saws and temporary work tables to cut mouldings, panels, gypsum, and other materials. If it's summertime and the weather is dry, sometimes a tradesperson can set up their equipment outside, but in urban areas there is a risk of theft and they can't operate outside if it rains. The garage makes the most logical temporary workshop. Thus, not only is the garage off limits for storage, you must take everything that you care about out, or at the end of the renovation it will be completely coated with sawdust. Don't keep strollers, kids' toys, clothing, or holiday decorations there or you will have a heck of a time cleaning everything off afterward. And DON'T expect the contractor or his tradesperson to remove everything at the beginning of the day before they start work and put it all back at the end of the day when they're done. You're paying them to renovate, not to be a moving service. It is, however, reasonable to ask and expect them to sweep the job site clean and pick up excess trash at the end of the day, and I recommend that you make that expectation clear at the outset.

How to responsibly dispose of your old stuff

Various charitable organizations will be happy to take your unwanted stuff and possibly even provide you with a tax receipt in return. Be aware however that due to rising labor and gas prices, charitable organizations often won't pick them up; you will have to arrange delivery to them. Or, if you'd rather, you can try to sell your things, either online, through a community newspaper, or at a garage sale.

When removing old kitchen cabinets and countertops, please do everything you can to keep them out of landfill sites. If they are in good condition, and you can't reuse them in a basement workshop, garage, or cottage, Habitat for Humanity has a ReStore, where they sell these kind of salvaged items and all the money goes to the organization's administrative costs, so all the proceeds from fundraising events can go to building decent housing for families in need.

In Canada, you can find Habitat for Humanity's Restore at:
http://www.habitat.ca/restoresc648.php

Habitat Restore directory for the USA:
http://www.habitat.org/cd/env/restore.aspx

You can also do an internet search on architectural salvage or take a photo before you demolish the kitchen and try to sell the whole thing on eBay or Craigslist. This way, if the items are in decent shape, you might even make a little money.

The other possibility is to do an online search for an auction house, which may be able to sell the items and pay you a portion of the price; alternatively, you could donate the proceeds to charity for a tax receipt.

Another idea is to do an online search for building surplus materials. One of these will provide the opportunity for you to keep your materials out of a landfill site. Although I have not tried this site myself, as another possibility, have a look at http://www.americanbuildersurplus.com/.

When the cabinets have been installed but you're waiting for two weeks for the stone counter top, it can be helpful if your contractor can install a temporary sink and even a piece of a laminate counter top so you can come up out of the basement.

The transformation from construction site to finished kitchen can take many weeks.

How Long Will It
Take? How Long?!
The Order of Work

HOW LONG WILL IT TAKE? HOW LONG?! THE ORDER OF WORK

Right after a new client asks "how much will it cost?" the very next question, invariably, is "how long will it take?" Often, the uninitiated is expecting to hear "a couple of weeks." When I tell them a couple of months, they become incredulous, until I explain what's involved.

Before anything starts, ask your designer, cabinet supplier, and your contractor for a meeting where you sit down together with a calendar and figure out a skeleton schedule of when everything should happen. When you know what the schedule should be, it's easier to cope with the disruption and mess. If you know what to expect, that's half the battle. Just be sure you don't get too attached to this timetable because it will inevitably be adjusted as you go along.

At this time, you'll also want to lay out the ground rules for working in your home and set a daily schedule for the tradespeople. If you are rushing around trying to get kids off to school before 8:00, you may not want to have workers invading your space until everyone is gone. If you can't always be there to let them in, you must give the contractor a key, so workers can come and go as needed. Keep in mind, if you make your schedule convenient for you but inconvenient for the work crew, your project will take longer and you will have difficulty getting some of the tradespeople to show up when they're needed.

Make it clear, preferably in your contract, that you expect someone to be working every day, and if they are not, they must call you to let you know. Things do happen, workers' illness or family duties, delayed deliveries, traffic accidents, all can upset even the most carefully planned schedule. But as long as you are kept informed, you must take this in stride. Nothing drives me crazier than when someone fails to show up and doesn't even have the courtesy to call! I regularly give this lecture to tradespeople, and unfortunately you will probably have to repeat it more than once before the job is done.

One thing you must accept and understand: it is highly unlikely that any tradesperson will work on the weekends. To you, your project is the most important thing going on in your life. To the workers, it is one of many and they need time with their families too. They work a five day week, just like most other people. In exceptional circumstances or when they're getting down to the last day before a deadline, then you may see a few people on the site on a weekend or evening, but don't count on it!

GET A PERMIT!

If you are moving a structural wall, you will need to have an engineer do a structural drawing, so it can be properly documented for a building permit application before doing any work. Removing a structural wall without a permit is very risky. If it isn't done properly and an accident happens, your insurance may not cover you. Also, in some areas, if you start work without a permit, and an inspector is alerted to your activities, they have the power to either stop construction until you get the proper documentation, or can even make you undo what you've already done and rebuild what was there before. Be safe. Get a permit.

Recently, I went to do a site visit at the home of a new client. They lived in a charming neighborhood featuring older homes and mature trees. They asked me to redesign the whole second floor, to enlarge the bathroom and get improved closet space. I knew something was wrong when I went upstairs and felt like I was going to slide from one end of the hall to the other because of a sloping floor! I went down to the main level to inspect the load-bearing wall underneath the upstairs hall, but there wasn't one! It had been removed by a previous owner without adding in the proper beams or posts to support the floor above. I really have no idea how the whole roof had not collapsed on their heads! So the first thing I did was call in the structural engineer to assess the situation. Needless to say, it turned into a much bigger project than they had anticipated!

The Schedule

For the purpose of illustrating a typical schedule, let's assume that you are removing a non load-bearing wall, removing existing soffits (called bulkheads in Canada), reconfiguring and replacing cabinets, countertop, flooring, and lighting in a room that is 12'-0" wide by 25'-0" long. Let's also assume that your cabinets will have crown moulding on top, light valance underneath the wall cabinets, granite countertop, new tile floors, and new pot lights that cannot be retrofitted into an existing ceiling.

Once the old wall board has been removed, the skeleton of the room will be exposed. This is one of the times the schedule may take a left turn as the contractor finds things in the walls that were unexpected.

Keep in mind this sample schedule is contingent on not having any unexpected surprises that may emerge when the construction begins.

Also be aware, when you see Day 1 and so on, these are not consecutive days, they are work days, Monday through Friday.

- **Day 1:** The day before the workers arrive (or however long you need), empty your cabinets and drawers and pack what you won't need for the next few months into boxes, and move what you will need to the area you've decided to use as your temporary kitchen. Move whatever appliances you can to that space as well. Try to borrow small appliances to help you prepare simple meals, like a toaster oven, electric kettle, electric frying pan, countertop grill, 2-burner electric hot plate, slow cooker, and the most important piece of survival equipment: a coffee maker!

- **Day 2:** The appliances will be disconnected and moved out of place, the plumbing will be disconnected, sink and faucet removed, the counters removed, and cabinets taken out or dismantled. If you have called a recycling company to take these things away, the items may have to sit in your garage or living room before they are picked up. Now that the room is empty, the contractor will strip the drywall from the wall that is slated for removal as well as the ceiling and the soffits. If there is time, the old flooring might also be torn up.

At this point, when the "skeleton" of the room is exposed, your contractor may discover some unforeseen issues that have to be handled, which might throw the schedule right out the window. Possible unwanted surprises include mold, faulty wiring, ancient, corroded plumbing, lack of insulation, or a compromised sub-floor. If this happens, he may have to fix the problem and reschedule the plumber and electrician. Depending on the

TALES FROM THE TRENCHES

Often in lower priced homes, there is a soffit running around the perimeter of the kitchen and the wall cabinets are installed tight up to the underside without crown moulding. This is a trick used by builders to keep costs down. Taller wall cabinets are more expensive. Also, a cabinet installed tight to the underside of a soffit doesn't need crown moulding which is typically an expensive accessory and is labor intensive to install. Each corner requires a mitred joint, and a bad installer will leave corners that don't meet properly. By eliminating the need for detailed work, a builder can use a less skilled laborer as well.

Most of the time the soffits are empty, but during a site measure, I will check the rooms above to ensure there are no floor registers which would indicate a duct in the soffit below, and to ensure there are no bathrooms directly over the kitchen which could point to plumbing in the soffit. If I'm still not sure, I'll have a contractor come in before I start designing and bash a hole in the soffit, stick a flashlight in it and look around. On occasion, I've seen an elbow of a pipe sticking down into the very back corner of the soffit. In this case, the soffit was used around the perimeter of the whole room to camouflage this one problematic corner. Always investigate the site thoroughly before the design is done, and the cabinets are ordered. Once the cabinets turn up on site, if there's an obstruction that can't be moved, the cabinets won't fit, and delays, extra costs and a huge amount of aggravation become inevitable.

schedule of their other jobs, you may have to wait for a break in the schedule for them to come back, causing a domino effect all the way down the line of tradespeople.

When the structure has been exposed, the contractor will also be able to see if there are any ducts or pipes or posts or other unforeseen obstructions which will make the wall removal and relocation more complicated. Once the site is swept, that may be pretty much it for the day. Although I've said this before, it bears repeating: I recommend that in your agreement with your contractor that you stipulate that the site must be swept clean at the end of the day and that no coffee cups or other trash is to be left lying around. It might be a construction site, but it's still your home.

In older homes, the structure may be lath and plaster rather than wall board. It doesn't necessarily need to be removed, but if the wiring is being updated it's preferable to clean it up with lumber and wall board that meets local building standards.

- **Days 3, 4, and 5:** We hope your contractor didn't find anything untoward when the kitchen got demolished, so the electrical and plumbing work can be started today on day three.

The plumbing relocation may be accomplished in one day, if it's a small job and the pipes in the basement are exposed and accessible, but the wiring will take a few days at least. Not only does the electrician have to remove the existing lights, he has to string wire to the locations of the new lights, connect it to the boxes (which are the guts of the new pot lights), run the wiring back to the breaker panel, and relocate receptacles and switches. Depending on your plan, he may also have to move phone jacks and TV cable outlets, and string new wire for the built-in speakers that go with your new kitchen stereo system. If it's an old home, he may have to update wiring to meet current building codes. The electrical work might also involve relocating intercom and security systems, which often require the vendors' contractors to come and do the work.

The electrician will use the manufacturer's specifications for the new appliances to determine where to relocate or add receptacles, and may have to run new wire back to the electrical panel if you are adding additional appliances like a steam oven, warming drawer, or wine fridge. This is also the time that the electrician will make sure that none of the breakers are being overloaded. If you've blown a breaker by plugging in a toaster and a kettle at the same time, even if they're in separate receptacles, it's because both those receptacles were wired back to the same breaker, and it is too heavy a load for the amperage, so the wiring has to be redistributed. If you have no empty breakers on your panel, the electrician will have to install an auxiliary panel (sometimes referred to as a pony panel) provided you have enough amperage coming into the house from the street. In new homes, 200 amp service is typical. In older homes, it's not uncommon to have only 100 amp service, which could mean you're going to be short on power if you plan to add heavy duty new appliances like a steam oven, speed oven, extra fridge, separate oven, or cook top.

While the electrician is doing his thing, the old wall studs have to be removed in the wall that is being eliminated.

- **Day 6:** If all has gone according to plan, the new wallboard might be able to go up today. That's pretty much a full day's work and not much else can happen in the room until that's done.

- **Days 7, 8, and 9:** The sheets of wallboard need to be taped at the seams and then a coat of drywall compound (often referred to as mud) is smoothed on top. When this is dry, it must be sanded and a new layer applied. This happens a few times, so that by the time the last layer of mud has been applied and sanded, the wallboard seams are invisible and there will be no bumps on the wall to mess up the paint job. Each coat of drywall mud must be dry and sanded before the new layer can be added, so there may be a few days where nothing else is happening in the room.

- **Day 10:** The wallboard on the ceiling will be cut out and at the location of the recessed lighting, wires will be pulled through for receptacles and switches.

- **Day 11:** Today a prime coat of paint will be put on the walls and ceiling.

- **Day 12:** If you've picked a paint color, a first coat can be applied to the walls today and a coat of ceiling paint can be done as well.

- **Day 13:** Today the new tile floor will be laid. First a layer of thinset mortar is spread on the sub floor and then the tiles are laid on top. They should be allowed to sit undisturbed for 24 hours before being walked on, so tiles don't move before they're set. Some of the electrical work can be done at the panel today if it is in a basement or utility room, as long as no one is in the kitchen.

  When the tile is laid, I always recommend that it goes down before the cabinets and gets installed right up to the walls so the new cabinets will sit on top of it. True, you are installing an extra 24" of tile around the perimeter of the room that won't be seen, but if you ever have a leak in the plumbing, it will cause less damage if the floor is completely sealed. It also provides a nice smooth surface for the cabinets to sit on.

  If you want to install radiant heat under your kitchen floor, it will be laid down before the thinset mortar goes down. There are a few different types of radiant heat: water pipes, electric coils, or mats. Depending on the type you're using, installation could add an additional day or two to the schedule. Be aware that using radiant heat makes your floor lovely and toasty warm on your bare feet, but you should not count on it as your main heat source in the room. If it were hot enough to heat the room, it would be too hot for the materials on the floor and the cabinetry sitting on top.

- **Day 14:** Nothing is happening today. The thinset under the tiles is drying, remember? Relax.

- **Day 15:** The tiles are grouted today. Relax some more. The cabinets should be coming tomorrow.

- **Day 16:** Provided all the materials have arrived in time and all the workers were able to complete their tasks with no major surprises, we're three weeks into the renovation and the cabinets should arrive today. The cabinet arrival and installation can be one of the most difficult elements to schedule. If your room preparation has been delayed for any reason that means the cabinet installation will have to be delayed. Typically, an installer's time is scheduled very tight. Depending on the length of the delay, he may have to go start another installation before your room is ready and come back when he can. This has an impact on all the other steps that have to be done in the kitchen, such as the countertop template, appliance installation, final coat of wall and ceiling paint, backsplash tiling, final plumbing, and electrical hook up.

If your cabinet supplier has ordered the cabinets for a "just-in-time" delivery and installation date, that means there's no leeway for delays. The safest way to order cabinets is to have them scheduled for delivery to a warehouse two weeks before the planned installation date, so that if there is a manufacturing delay, it won't hold up progress on the site. This, however, requires more coordination and paying a storage fee which may not be feasible on your project. As a result, this may be simply where you keep your fingers and toes crossed.

When you sign the contract for your cabinet purchase, I recommend that you stipulate that the packing materials are to be removed from the job site and disposed of as part of the purchase price. Otherwise, you might be left with a mountain of cardboard, packing tape, packing foam, or other packing material. If you have ordered your cabinets from a local custom shop, you may be receiving cabinets that have just been blanket-wrapped for delivery, which is obviously the most eco-conscious way to do it, but not practical if the cabinets are traveling a long distance.

A good installer who is taking care to ensure your cabinets are level and plumb will take a week or a little more to finish, longer if it's an elaborate design, has custom pieces to assemble on site, or if there are complicated mouldings to cut and install.

- *Day 17:* Have the appliances delivered today. I recommend that you have the appliances on site for the cabinet installation, so their sizes can be confirmed before the cabinets are in place. Appliance specifications can change without warning, and if you bought a range that you thought required a 30" width and it actually requires 30 ¼" you would have a disaster on your hands if the appliances showed up after the cabinets were in.

I suggest that you arrange to have the appliances delivered the day after the cabinet installation starts. That way, the installer will have placed the base cabinets but won't yet have attached anything to the wall, so there will be a little bit of space in the room for the appliances, and he can place the appliances where they ought to go if they are freestanding models, or if they are built-in models, he can measure them to ensure he leaves enough space for them in the cabinet layout.

- **Day 18:** The cabinet installation continues. If you have no fancy base columns or pilasters, perhaps by the end of today the base cabinets will be fastened in place.

- **Day 19:** Once the base cabinets have been permanently fastened in place, you can have the countertop people come in to do a template. This is required for all stone, man-made solid material tops, and I recommend it even for laminate tops. The countertop installer will come in and measure the base cabinet installation

and compare it to the drawing your designer sent him to check for discrepancies, and depending on the company, he will use a digital recorder or will take a physical template using large sheets of cardboard laid on top of the base cabinets and marked and cut so they are the exact size and shape of the finished countertops. These will be taken back to the shop and laid on a slab of stone and traced, so the stone can be cut to size. The countertop template measurer also will require the appliances as well as the sink and even the faucet to be on site too. Some countertop fabricators will want to take your sink back to their shop to cut out the hole there, while some will just take the sink template out of the box and use that. Either way is acceptable. Less acceptable in my opinion is cutting out the hole for the sink on the job site. It is a messy job with copious amounts of potentially toxic dust contaminating the air in the home. Furthermore, if you are using an under-mount sink (the edge of it is siliconed to the underside of the countertop rather than sitting on the surface like a top-mount sink), the edge of the cutout will have to be perfect and polished, which is not easy, if not impossible, to accomplish on the job site.

- **Days 20, 21, 22, and 23:** The wall cabinet installation may be started today. If you have a single installer with no helper, a wall cabinet installation is a difficult task to do well. A European cabinet system has a metal hanging rail that must be attached to the wall first. As long as it is level, the wall cabinets, which have a corresponding hook rail on the back of them, can just be hung on the rail and then screwed into the studs and to each other to create a permanent installation. However, if your cabinets are custom made or made in North America in a more traditional way (the Europeans call it old fashioned), they need to be lifted up to their required height and location and held in place while they are screwed to the wall. It is helpful to have four arms for this job, but if you have a single installer, he will have to rely on gadgetry designed to lift the cabinets. It works. It just takes longer than if you have two pairs of hands. Once the wall cabinets are in place, any specialty mouldings like crown, corbels, pilasters, decorative feet, legs, or appliqués will be assembled and installed. Shelves will be put in and adjusted, doors will be hung and adjusted, and handles or knobs attached. This last little detail can take longer than you think. If you are installing the same knob on every door and drawer, it's fairly straightforward for the installer to create a jig to ensure that the knobs go in the same place on each door and drawer face. If however, you're doing something interesting like using knobs on the doors and handles on the drawers, or different sized handles on every size of drawer, the drilling for this is a painstaking affair. Each handle has to be measured and placed according to each size door and drawer. You may find it hard to believe that this one task can take pretty much a whole day. The rule of thumb is anything that looks really interesting usually takes longer to install.

If the cabinet toe kick (the recessed flat panels that go from the floor to the underside of the base cabinets) hasn't gone in before now, it can be done today.

- **Day 24 through 29:** Now that the cabinets are pretty much completely installed, you might reasonably think that the countertop would be installed today, right?

Wrong. It typically takes about 10 working days from the time a countertop template is done to the time that the countertop comes back to be installed. During that time some of the appliances might be able to be installed, like the fridge and the wall oven and microwave, but since no one likes to make two trips to a job site if they can do it in one, more than likely the appliances will still be sitting waiting for the countertops to go in first.

The other things that can be done while you're waiting for the countertops to come are finishing the baseboard around the room, the door, and window trim. Often these mouldings are given a primer and first coat of paint before it is cut and installed so the finish coat can be applied more easily and quickly.

The painter may also want to do touch ups in areas where the countertop will not be going...although as per the comment above about not wanting to go to a site twice if one trip can be made, the painter might prefer to wait and do everything at once.

- **Day 30:** Yippee! Today the countertop is coming! The end is in sight, right? Not so fast... A stone countertop installation will take several hours. Slabs weighing a couple hundred pounds are not easy to maneuver out of the truck, into the house, and onto the cabinets. There will be at least two if not three people needed to do this job. Since stone is usually sold in slabs that are a maximum of 5' wide by 10' long, almost all countertops will have seams in several different locations. If you have a really good stone fabricator, they know how to minimize the number of seams and locate them where they will be least visible but they will always be visible. One of these seams may be at the sink cut out, since most of the seam is cut away for the sink hole.

Once two adjoining slabs are in place, the seam has to be filled. Sometimes it is grouted like a tile and sometimes a silicone adhesive is used. Like most things in life, both these materials have advantages and disadvantages. Grout is subject to cracking if the floor settles and the cabinets shift slightly. Silicone will eventually start to peel away, but it's then fairly easy to dig out, clean up, and reapply.

If you are doing an under-mount sink, it will be fastened in place with silicone and temporarily braced from underneath for 24 hours until the silicone has set, after which the plumbing can be hooked up.

- **Day 31:** Today the plumbing gets hooked up, and the appliances can be installed. You might also see the electrician who will now be able to hook up the under cabinet lighting. (It is my very special pet peeve that this is often referred to as under counter lighting. It is not under the counter, it is under the wall cabinet which lights up the counter.) We wait until after the countertops are installed to put in the under cabinet lights since the counters are so difficult to manoeuvre and if a corner accidentally hits the under cabinet light, you will have a broken fixture and a problem to deal with. Better to wait and do it properly. For the same reason, we wait to install a pendant light fixture over the island.

- **Day 32:** The backsplash material is installed today. But as with the floor, if you are using tiles of any description, they first have to be stuck on the wall and the adhesive has to dry before grouting. If you are using slabs of mirror or glass, no grout is required. Ensure that enough tile has been ordered particularly if it's a custom order as with many type of glass tile. Normally 10% more than you need will cover the waste required for cutting or damage. But for a complex pattern, as much as 20% could be required.

- **Day 33:** The backsplash tile is grouted. Now the electrician can put all the receptacle and switch plates on.

- **Day 34:** The final coat of paint can be applied today after the cabinets and crown moulding have been protected with painter's tape.

Summing up the schedule

So here we are, seven weeks after we started the demolition of the old kitchen, the new kitchen is in and ready to use. Now here comes the big BUT…

This schedule assumes that nothing has gone wrong, there have been no mistakes, everyone has shown up exactly when they were scheduled and all the materials arrived on time. A project in real life almost never happens that way. If a tradesperson (who is always working on another job when he's not at your house), is held up on another job by something that takes him longer than he planned or by some other delay or emergency, he may not turn up at your house when he was scheduled. This means that everyone else who needed him to complete his work before they could start theirs is going to be held up too which is why there may be days here and there when no one is working in your house. It is as frustrating for the workers as it is for you since their schedule is always being changed on them and they have to scramble to readjust. To be safe and not be disappointed, you should expect to add at least 10 to 15 extra working days to this schedule for this type of eventuality. So, like I said at the beginning, it will take a couple of months. Do you believe me now?!

This odd little kitchen was in two separate rooms, so removing the non-load bearing wall improved the flow and function.
Read the whole story of *"The Little Kitchen That Could"* on my blog at www.RenovationBootcamp.com.

Before and After

DONATO

Why Does It Take So Long To Finish The Last Few Things?

WHY DOES IT TAKE SO LONG TO FINISH THE LAST FEW THINGS?

As was discussed in the previous chapter, there is the possibility that some materials are delayed or, heaven forbid, someone makes an ordering mistake and an item comes in the wrong colors, shape, or size. If this happens, the item in question will have to be re-ordered. Sometimes, depending on the item and the relationship between the vendor and the person who originally ordered it, it could possibly be expedited; however, you might still wait a few weeks. Once the piece comes in, it has to be delivered and installed. That's where the real hold up could occur. It could take a couple of weeks to get an installer to come back, so you might end up waiting for five weeks overall for one or two pieces to get finished.

Find it hard to believe? Let me walk you through it…

Let's say a cabinet was manufactured in the wrong size, which you won't find out until it arrives at the job site and the installer goes to put it in place (This is less of a possibility with a custom cabinet maker who is building each cabinet to order. It occasionally happens with a large manufacturer where an order processor types orders into a computerized system. One typo and you could receive a cabinet that is 36" wide instead of 36" tall.) At that point, someone has to re-order the cabinet.

The replacement order has to be written up and then sent to the manufacturer, who typically sends back an acknowledgement. Once the dealer checks the acknowledgement and confirms, the order goes into production. This process alone could take up to a few days of back and forth communication, provided everyone gets to it immediately. Once the order goes into production, some manufacturers have a policy of putting what are called "service parts" at the front of the production line. However, that's not always possible, and you may have to wait several weeks for the order sitting in a queue before the part is made. Then it has to be delivered. That was the easy part. You are now at the mercy of the installer's schedule. The installer will almost certainly be working on another job and he can't leave to come finish yours. He has to have a break in his schedule first. If the cabinet that was the wrong size was in a critical place where there was plumbing or something else that depended on its installation, the delays, and difficulties compound further.

The example above is an illustration of why finishing off a project can be the longest, most time consuming, and painful part of the whole process. So many people depend on one another to do their part that it can seem to take forever to get the last few things done at a time when you want nothing more than to have every stranger out of your home and to enjoy your new kitchen with your family. This is where the quality of your designer/project manager/contractor is critical. If they have efficient processes and procedures, the delays can be minimized. If they don't, it will seem like a comedy of errors before the project is done. No matter how frustrating or painful it gets, this is where you need to take a very, very deep breath and have a good laugh about it all. Like giving birth to a beautiful baby, it will all be worth it in the end.

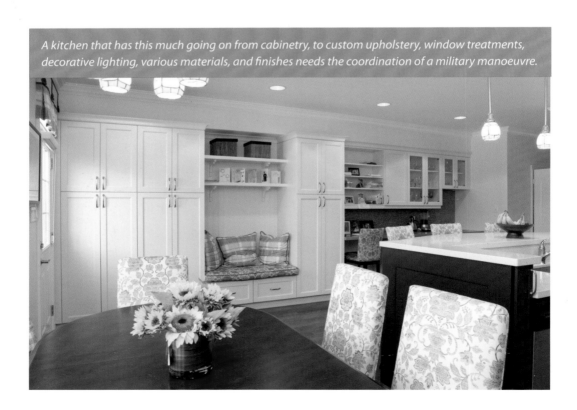

A kitchen that has this much going on from cabinetry, to custom upholstery, window treatments, decorative lighting, various materials, and finishes needs the coordination of a military manoeuvre.

In almost 20 years in this business, I have worked with many different types of cabinet makers, from custom shops to international manufacturers. One of the challenges in working with an international manufacturer can be a language issue.

Over the years I have been a cabinet dealer for various manufacturers whose first language was different from mine. I would do the drawings, write up the order, which listed every single part, its color, shape, and size, and sent it in to the order processing department. At that time the manufacturer's order processor was still only accepting orders via fax, so they had to re-type my written order and input it into their computer system. It was so critical that the order was perfect, that when they sent the acknowledgement back to us, it went through three proofreading checks with three different people, to make sure there were no errors. We would usually find at least two or three mistakes. We would make the corrections and send it back. They would correct it at their end and send it back again. This back and forth could happen 3 times over a period of two weeks before we were finally able to approve the order for production.

On one occasion, after having gone through this procedure, the day of the cabinet delivery arrived, and I was confident that we would have a perfect installation, since I knew that the order had been submitted without errors. It was not a complex design, so given that the order was correct, that should have been the case. However, when the installer started the job, he discovered that of the two pantries that were to be installed side by side, one was 3 inches shorter than the other! I scrambled through the files to check the written order and it had been correct...no size discrepancy there. I then flew through the acknowledgements to check whether we had missed something in the translation. Nope, everything had been fine there too. Then how the heck could this have happened? Being human, someone in the factory read the order incorrectly and made the pantry the wrong height. This took four weeks to remedy; from the time we placed the remedial order, it finally was delivered and installed. Fortunately everything else could be completed while we waited. We had the plumbing hooked up, the electrical done and all the appliances were functional, but our client still had her food in boxes until the correctly sized pantry arrived. There was nothing anyone could do to make it go faster. So, remember, if this happens to you, yelling, screaming, and stamping your feet seldom helps.

Putting Your
Dishes Away

PUTTING YOUR DISHES AWAY

Food for thought:

"Cleaning your house while your kids are still growing is like shoveling the sidewalk before it stops snowing."
- Phyllis Diller

When the last tradesperson leaves the building, you may hear angels singing and run to the boxes to put the dishes away.

STOP!!!

You absolutely have to clean the cabinets properly before you put away one dish.

Now, this may seem like a totally dumb, obvious thing to say, but you would be amazed at the number of people who take a damp cloth and wave it around the cabinets and proceed to put their stuff away.

Bad idea. A thin layer of toxic dust which is very difficult to see inhabits your new cabinets, inside and out. To either inhale or ingest this dust is dangerous, so if your budget allows, please have a professional cleaning service come in to do a final "renovation clean," stipulate that they not only have to clean the outsides of the cabinets, but they have to clean the tops and undersides of every single shelf, the side walls, ceiling and floor of every single cabinet, the doors (making sure to clean all the crevices of the door design), the exterior cabinet walls, and the mouldings. They also need to wipe down the walls; the ceiling and the floor should be washed at least twice. Construction dust is notoriously difficult to eliminate. Because it's so fine, a first cleaning can still leave a film of dust which, when it dries, becomes airborne via the heating and cooling system.

When doing the cleaning, you should use non-toxic cleaners (no ammonia, bleach, detergents with phosphates, or other hazardous substances), and replace cleaning water with fresh water frequently, or you will just end up pushing the dust around.

If your house has forced-air gas heating, the other thing you must do is hire a professional company to clean your ducts. The sawdust, drywall dust, and bits and pieces of building material invariably fall down into the floor registers. As your furnace or air conditioner pushes air back up into the house, much of this dust circulates back into the atmosphere for you to breathe. Cleaning your ducts may also increase the efficiency of your heating and cooling equipment by improving air flow.

Recent studies show more people, particularly children, are exhibiting signs of breathing problems like asthma and bronchitis than in previous generations. Many scientists blame indoor air quality in our homes, which is often many times more polluted than the air outside! This is due to a combination of factors, including fumes from toxic cleaning products, air fresheners, and the off-gassing of various materials including building materials, glues, carpets, fabrics, and paints.

To minimize these hazards as much as possible, the cleaning step cannot be over emphasized. It should not be downplayed or glossed over, and I recommend you use products that are as eco-friendly as possible.

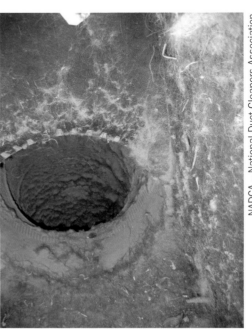

Cleaning the ducts after a major renovation is a good idea. Fine toxic dust from the construction can settle in the ducts and then get blown back into the atmosphere which can aggravate allergies and breathing problems.

NADCA – National Duct Cleaners Association

Have a glass of wine & relax

(or start planning the bathroom project!)

Now that the job is all done and you're moved back into your kitchen, you can start putting all the renovation anxiety behind you and enjoy the space to create meals and memories with your friends and family.

However, you'll want to remain friends with your cabinet supplier and installer, because you're going to have to have them back at least once more before they are but a distant memory.

If you used granite or some other dense stone or man-made composite material for your countertops, you've added 300 to 500 pounds of weight onto the cabinets. Don't be surprised if the drawers in your base cabinets start rubbing, and the doors look crooked. The weight of the countertop is causing the cabinets to settle, and the drawer glides and door hinges may have to be adjusted. Not to worry, it's a simple fix since most hardware is adjustable in a couple of different directions.

After that, there is nothing left but to enjoy a long and happy life in your kitchen.

Cheers!

"Now ...about that bathroom..."

RENOVATION BOOTCAMP™:

Kitchen Use and Needs Audit.
© Robin Siegerman 2011

Appendix A:

When you start thinking about remodeling your kitchen, it will help everyone involved if you are really clear about what you want, why you want it, how you use it, and when you want it done. This gets more detailed than you may expect, so here's a questionnaire that will help you clarify your priorities and will be immeasurably helpful to the people who are helping you design and construct your dream kitchen.

Date:	
Site address:	
What is your project budget?	
When do you want to start the project?	
By what date do you hope to have it completed?	
Is this project for new construction or renovation?	
If it's for a renovation, are you doing the project for resale or to improve the quality of life in your home?	
How long have you lived in the house?	
How long do you envision staying in the house?	
Who will live in the house with you (names and ages)?	

Do you have outside people working in the kitchen (i.e. nanny, housekeeper, regular babysitter, cook, caterer)? **List them and how many times a week they are there:**	
Does anyone in the home have any disabilities or serious allergies? **List and explain:**	
What do you dislike most about your current kitchen that should be avoided in the new kitchen?	
Do you like bright lighting?	
Do you want the ability to dim the lights?	
Do you want any decorative lighting (i.e. pendent fixture over an island or table)?	
Do you grow plants such as herbs in the kitchen that need special lighting?	
Do you have pets that need to live in the kitchen?	
List their names, ages and species (i.e. dog, cat, rabbit, guinea pig, etc.):	
Who is the main cook?	
Does more than one person use the kitchen to prepare food simultaneously?	
Are they right- or left-handed?	
How tall are they?	
How many times a week do you prepare a family meal from scratch?	
Does anyone come home for lunch?	

Do you make a lunch for family members to take to work or school? If yes, how many people?	
How do you shop - weekly, daily, in bulk?	
Do you buy a lot of canned or boxed goods, prepared or frozen foods, or mostly fresh?	
Which types of cooking do you do most of the time (i.e. stir fry, casseroles, slow cooker meals, frozen food/reheating, ordering in, desserts)?	
Do you need a large amount of spice storage? Or condiment storage? How many bottles do you have now vs. how many you would like to have in the new kitchen?	
How many cookbooks do you want to keep in the kitchen? Do you want them visible, on open shelves, or behind a door (if they are tattered and well-loved)?	
Do you bake? How often?	
Do you bake your own pastries or use a mix or frozen? **Do you roll a lot of pastry?**	
What small appliances would you like to incorporate into your new kitchen? (i.e. toaster, toaster oven, rice cooker, slow cooker, electric kettle, coffee maker, pasta maker, bread maker, griddle/grill, stand mixer, food processor, blender) **List them and their approximate sizes:**	
What activities take place in the kitchen besides cooking? (i.e. paying bills, computer games, watching TV, homework, crafts, laundry)	

Do you want a desk or message centre in the kitchen?	
Do you want wireless internet hub to be in the kitchen?	
Do you need more than one phone line?	
Do you want to incorporate a fireplace?	
Do you want a TV or stereo?	
Do you want a family room type seating area in the kitchen?	
Do you want to eat in the kitchen? If so, how many have to be seated there?	
Do you have a strong preference as to whether the eating area is at counter height (36" high) or bar height (41" high) or does it have to be at table height?	
If space and budget allows, which large appliances do you want? (state size and manufacturer preference, i.e. Kitchen Aid 36" fridge etc)	
Fridge (built-in, counter depth, French door, freezer on top or bottom, drawers):	
Dishwasher (European size, apartment size, North American size, or drawers):	
Wall oven (single or double):	
Cook top (halogen, induction, gas, or electric coil):	
Side-in range (gas or electric top):	
Drop-in range (gas or electric top):	
Microwave (with convection capabilities or not):	
Warming drawer:	

Steam oven:	
Speed oven:	
Built-in coffee/cappuccino maker:	
Deep fryer:	
Beverage fridge:	
Wine cooler:	
Washer/dryer:	
Do you want any special items on display (i.e. dishes, family heirlooms, photos)?	
What do you want the cabinets to look like (show photographs pulled out of magazines)? Do you want the cabinet finish to be wood-stained, painted, laminate, or metal?	
Which cabinet accessories do you want to incorporate? (Use a checkmark for yes, X for no):	
Tray/baking pan divider storage	
Pot drawers	
Spice storage	
Roll out shelves	
Rotating corner shelves or other corner solutions	
Pull out towel bar	
Recycling/compost bins	
Waste bins	
Wine storage	
Carving knife storage	

Glass doors	
Type of glass (i.e. stained, frosted, clear, antique, textured)	
Cutlery dividers	
Utensil dividers	
Backsplash accessory hanging rail	
Chopping block	
Swing up food processor shelf	
Appliance garage	
Bread box	
Pull out baskets	
File drawer	
Keyboard pull out shelf	
Broom cabinet fittings	
Toe kick step ladder	
What type of flooring are you thinking of using?	
What type of material are you leaning towards for the countertop (i.e. granite, marble, laminate, wood, quartz, solid, surface, etc.)?	
Would you prefer a double bowl sink, single, or 1 1/2?	
Do you ever need a dish drainer on the counter?	
Would you want a second sink somewhere else in the kitchen?	
What kind of faucet do you prefer (i.e. two-handled, single lever, pull out spray head, touch control)?	

What do you envision on the backsplash (i.e. stone, ceramic or glass tile, granite or other stone slab, glass, mirror, metal)?	
How often do you entertain?	
How many people at a time do you typically entertain?	
Do you have large family gatherings in your home?	
Do you hire catering staff?	
Is your entertaining casual or formal?	
How many events of each would you have per month?	
Do you want to remove any walls? **Explain:**	
Are you thinking of adding an addition to the house?	
Do you need to add or replace existing windows?	
Do you want to add or replace a skylight?	
Do you want to add or replace an exterior door?	
Is there more than one kitchen in the house?	
Do you have a large, chest-type or upright freezer in the house now, or do you want to add one?	

Additional thoughts or notes:

_8_

SHOPPING LIST:

Kitchen Use and Needs Audit.
© Robin Siegerman 2011

This will help you remember what you looked at and help your kitchen designer know your preferences. Make as many copies as you need, so you can have a fresh one for each vendor you visit. TAKE A TAPE MEASURE WITH YOU!

APPLIANCES	
Store Name:	
Date Visited:	
Address:	
Phone:	
Web site:	
E-mail:	
Salesperson's Name:	
Is installation included in the price?	
Is delivery included in the price?	
Will the delivery people take away the packing materials?	
APPLIANCES YOU LOOKED AT:	
FRIDGE	
Brand	
Model #	

Water line required (for automatic ice maker or cold water)	
Do you want cabinet match panel on the front?	
Built-in, slide in, or free standing	
Exterior dimensions (height to top of hinge)	
Color	
Lead time	
Price	
RANGE	
Brand	
Model #	
Drop-in, slide-in, free standing	
Gas, electric, or induction cooking surface	
Exterior dimensions	
Color	
Lead time	
Price	
COOK TOP (if separate from the oven)	
Brand	
Model #	
Flush mount, surface mount, or break front (protrudes beyond the counter top edge)	
Glass, coil, gas, induction	

Exterior dimensions	
Color	
Lead time	
Price	
WALL OVEN (if separate from the cook top)	
Brand	
Model #	
Double or single	
Gas or electric	
Exterior dimensions	
Color	
Lead time	
Price	
MICROWAVE	
Brand	
Model#	
Convection (yes/no)	
Regular hinge, drop down door, or drawer model	
Exterior dimensions	
Color	
Lead time	
Price	
DISHWASHER	
Brand	
Model #	

Regular hinge or drawers	
Color	
Do you want cabinet match panel on the front	
Lead time	
Price	
WARMING DRAWER	
Brand	
Model #	
Do you want a cabinet match panel on the front	
Exterior dimensions	
Lead time	
Price	
BEVERAGE FRIDGE	
Brand	
Model #	
Color	
Do you want a cabinet match panel on the front	
Exterior dimensions	
Lead time	
Price	
WINE COOLER	
Brand	
Model #	

Color	
Do you want a cabinet match panel on the front	
Exterior dimensions	
Lead time	
Price	
BUILT-IN COFFEE MAKER	
Brand	
Model #	
Water line required	
Exterior dimensions	
Lead time	
Price	
STEAM OVEN	
Brand	
Model #	
Water line required	
Exterior dimensions	
Lead time	
Price	
DEEP FRYER	
Brand	
Model #	
Exterior Dimensions	
Lead time	
Price	

CLOTHES WASHER	
Brand	
Model #	
Under counter, stacking, or free-standing, front or top loading	
Exterior Dimensions	
Color	
Lead time	
Price	
CLOTHES DRYER	
Brand	
Model #	
Front or top loading or stackable	
Exterior vent or vent-less	
Exterior dimensions	
Color	
Lead time	
Price	

OTHER APPLIANCES NOT LISTED ABOVE

CABINETRY	

If you ask these questions of each cabinet supplier you visit, you'll be able to compare the services each company offers and assess which one will suit your needs best.

Date	
Vendor visited (kitchen dealer/designer)	
Contact person's name	

Address	
Phone number, web address, e-mail	
How many years have they been in business?	
Do they price their cabinets by linear foot?	
If not, can they give you a ball park estimate before doing a design?	
How much do they charge to do a design?	
Is the designer a Certified Kitchen Designer or Registered/ Licensed Interior Designer?	
What happens if you don't like the first design, do they have a limit on how many changes they will make for the design fee?	
What kind of drawings can you expect to see?	
Do you get to keep the drawings before you place a cabinet order?	
Does the design fee get applied to the price of the cabinets when you make a deposit?	
Once the design has been done and approved and you choose a material, stain or paint color, and door style, will they be able to lend out samples, so you can take them shopping to help you pick out counter top colors, backsplash tiles, flooring, and fabric?	

What are the payment terms?	
Is there a warranty?	
What is the delivery lead time?	
Can you see a copy of their contract?	
Who installs the cabinets?	
Does the same installer return to do any service work required?	
Do they also sell sinks, faucets, countertops, backsplash tiles?	
Will their employees or sub-contractor install the pieces above, or do you have to hire an outside contractor do that?	
CABINET DETAILS DISCUSSED	
Door Style	
Overall height of cabinets	
Door Material (wood, veneer, MDF, laminate)	
Cabinet box construction (particle board, plywood)	
Cabinet box construction (dowel, glue, nail, staple)	
Self-closing hardware on doors and drawers	
Handles or knobs chosen	
INTERNAL ACCESSORIES LOOKED AT:	
Roll out shelves	
Trash/recycling composting system	

Toe kick step ladder	
Cutlery and utensil trays	
Carving knife drawer insert	
Spice storage	
Chopping block	
Towel bars, holders, pullouts	
Pot drawers	
Tray dividers	
Pantry shelf systems (bottle holders on the doors, swing out shelves)	
Corner cabinet solutions (i.e. full or half rotating shelves, magic corner swing out hardware, corner drawers)	
Glass door display cabinets	
Cleaning product storage	
Broom closet accessories	
Cook books storage	
Computer keyboard pull out	
COUNTER TOPS	
Date	
Vendor	
Contact person's name	
Address	
Web site	
E-mail	

Materials looked at, color name and number:	
Granite	
Marble	
Limestone	
Laminate	
Quartz (Zodiac®, HanStone®, Caesarstone®, Silestone®, IceStone®, Cambria®, etc)	
Solid Surface (Corian®, Gibralter®, Avonite Surfaces™, etc)	
Paperstone®	
Did you get samples?	
What edge thickness do you want?	
What edge profile do you prefer?	
What is the typical lead time between the time the counter top is templated/measured and installed?	
Does the cabinet installer have to provide a template or will the counter top vendor do that?	
Does the material require a sealant?	
How often does it need to be done?	
Will the vendor add the sealant that the first time?	
Do they sell sealant for subsequent applications?	
What are the payment terms?	
Is there a warranty offered?	

BACKSPLASH MATERIALS	
Date	
Vendor	
Contact Name:	
Address	
Web site	
E-mail	
Materials looked at, size, color name, and number:	
Ceramic tile	
Glass tile	
Stone tile	
Slab of glass	
Mirror	
Metal	
Grout color	
Does the vendor sell the mortar as well?	
Do they do installations?	
If not, can they recommend an installer who is familiar with this type of product?	
What are the vendor's payment terms?	
How far in advance does the product need to be ordered?	

FLOORING	
Date	
Vendor	
Contact Name:	
Address	
Web site	
E-mail	
Materials looked at, size, color name, and number:	
Ceramic tile	
Glass tile	
Stone tile	
Glass tile	
Cork tile	
Cork plank	
Wood (oak, maple, cherry, walnut, etc.)	
Vinyl (tile or sheet)	
Laminate	
Does the vendor install the product or can they recommend a qualified installer?	
Is there a warranty?	
How far in advance does the material need to be ordered?	
What are the vendor's payment terms?	

PLUMBING FIXTURES & FAUCETS	
Date	
Vendor	
Contact Name:	
Address	
Web site	
E-mail	
Items looked at, size, color name, and number:	
Stainless steel	
Copper	
Ceramic	
Cast iron	
Stone	
Resin	
Kitchen sink (single bowl, 1 1/2 bowl)	
Style (undermount, top mount, apron front)	
Bar or prep sink (round, square, rectangle, top mount, undermount)	
Kitchen sink faucet (pull out spray head, separate sprayer, 2-handle, single lever, chrome, stainless steel, brushed nickel)	
Bar sink faucet (cold water only, cold and hot, single leaver, 2-handle, goose neck, chrome, stainless steel, brushed nickel)	

LIGHTING	
Date	
Vendor	
Contact Name:	
Address	
Web site	
E-mail	
Items looked at, height, width, color, material, brand, model #:	
Pendant fixture	
Ceiling flush mount	
Semi-flush mount	
Under cabinet lighting	
Pot lights	
How far in advance do the fixtures need to be ordered?	
What are the vendor's payment terms?	
What is the vendor's return policy?	
Can they recommend a licensed electrician?	

MEASURING TEMPLATE:

Appendix C:

Kitchen Use and Needs Audit.
© Robin Siegerman 2011

Once you're ready to set out on your product reconnaissance missions, it would be useful not only to bring your tape measure, but a dimensioned sketch of your kitchen as well. Although a kitchen designer will have to do a detailed measure of your home before composing any detailed drawings, in your initial discussions, it will help if they can get a visual sketch of the space you have to work with and its size. They might even be able to give you a rough estimate of costs. Be as accurate as you can and try not to round your dimensions up or down. Don't worry about drawing it to scale, the designer will take care of that. All you have to do is provide reasonably accurate dimensions.

Here's a summary of what you want to measure. The plan below will help you visualize exactly what I'm talking about:

Total room length and width (in INCHES)	
Ceiling height	
Width of door and window trim	
Height of ceiling cornice moulding if applicable	
Width of the door and window openings	
Dimensions of wall widths between door and window openings	
Note if there are any soffits or bulkheads running around the perimeter of the room at the ceiling line and how high it is (this might determine the height of the wall cabinets)	

Indicate a North wall	
Indicate which kitchen doorways lead to other rooms.	
It would be helpful to indicate the general location of any heat supply registers	

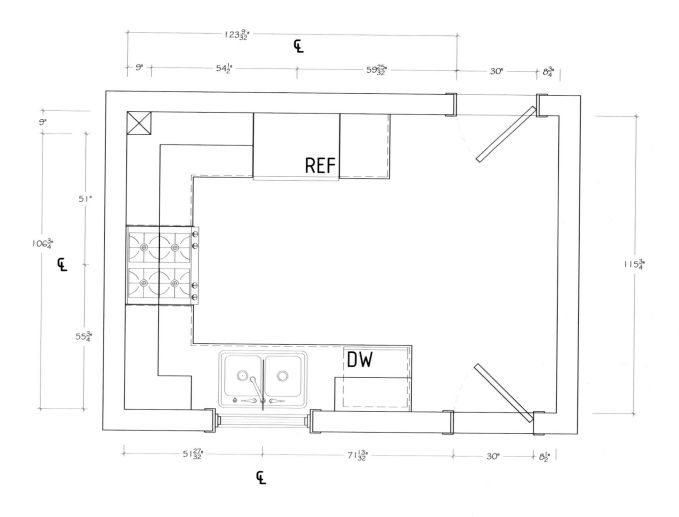

RENOVATION BOOTCAMP ACKNOWLEGEMENTS

The time between the first thought of, "Hey! I'm gonna write a book!" and the final product is a longer adventure than I ever imagined, but it was made much smoother and less lonely with help from many:

Thanks to my good friend Steve Thomas for writing the foreword. When I first met Steve and his delightful wife Evy on the slopes of Alta, Utah, many years ago, I couldn't have imagined that we would have so much in common. Talking "shop" is just one of the pleasures when we find ourselves in the same city, and I value their friendship.

Heaps of gratitude to Andy Donato for his wit and talent found in the cartoons. Also, many thanks for your patience!

Teresa Toten, author, wonderful client, and writing mentor who slogged through my first draft and gave me invaluable feedback, I so appreciate your support and encouragement.

Robin Hoffman whose eyes and editing skills have no doubt saved me from myself.

Leslee Mason, Editor of Canadian Kitchen & Bath, with whom I traded cryptic "bon mots" when I wrote the Designer to Designer column, has given me some excellent comments both for the column and the book. Write on, Leslee!

Thanks to Robert Caplan of Caplan's Appliances for professional support and being the eyes for the appliance information and Harold Hartmann who vetted the chapter on lighting.

Thanks to Ray Wilkins for "getting it" with the cover design.

Thanks to the great folks at Yorkshire Publishing, particularly Lily, Luke, & Todd! Wow, quite an experience, eh?!

Thanks to Peggy McColl and Steve Harrison for putting information on writing, publishing, and promoting into the universe which convinced me that I could embark on such an audacious journey! Their expertise and integrity have been my inspiration.

To all my clients who have graciously shared intimate details of their lives which allowed me to design and renovate their kitchens: I thank you and wish you good friends, good food, and good life in your kitchens!

And last but definitely not least, thanks to my husband Steve (the Uzi in Sieguzi!), and my son Julian (who makes me proud every day), both of whom have tolerated the hours spent glued to my computer and my occasional writing rants, but have consistently encouraged and supported this "crazy book thing."